Bushwhacking on a Grand Scale

THE BATTLE OF CHICKAMAUGA, SEPTEMBER 18-20, 1863

By William Lee White

EMERGING CIVIL WAR SERIES

Chris Mackowski, series editor
Kristopher D. White, historical content editor

Also part of the Emerging Civil War Series:

Bloody Autumn: The 1864 Valley Campaign
    by Daniel T. Davis and Phillip Greenwalt

Grant's Last Battle: The Story Behind the Personal Memoirs
of Ulysses S. Grant
    by Chris Mackowski and Kristopher D. White

The Last Days of Stonewall Jackson: The Mortal Wounding
of the Confederacy's Greatest Icon
    by Chris Mackowski and Kristopher D. White

A Season of Slaughter: The Battle of Spotsylvania Court House, May 8-21, 1864
    by Chris Mackowski and Kristopher D. White

Simply Murder: The Battle of Fredericksburg, December 13, 1862
    by Chris Mackowski and Kristopher D. White

Also by this Author:

Great Things Are Expected of Us: The Letters of Colonel C. Irvine Walker, 10th South
Carolina Infantry CSA
    William Lee White, editor

Bushwhacking on a Grand Scale

THE BATTLE OF CHICKAMAUGA, SEPTEMBER 18-20, 1863

By William Lee White

EMERGING CIVIL WAR SERIES

SB

Savas Beatie

California

First edition, first printing 2013

ISBN-13: 978-1-61121-158-0

Library of Congress Cataloging-in-Publication Data

White, William Lee.
Bushwhacking on a grand scale : the Battle of Chickamauga, September 18-20, 1863 / by William L. White.
pages cm
Includes bibliographical references.
ISBN 978-1-61121-158-0
1. Chickamauga, Battle of, Ga., 1863. I. Title.
E475.81.W56 2013
973.7'359--dc23
2013033248

SB

Published by
Savas Beatie LLC
989 Governor Drive, Suite 102
El Dorado Hills, California 95762
Phone: 916-941-6896
Email: sales@savasbeatie.com
Web: www.savasbeatie.com

Savas Beatie titles are available at special discounts for bulk purchases in the United States by corporations, institutions, and other organizations. For more details, please contact Special Sales, P.O. Box 4527, El Dorado Hills, CA 95762, or you may e-mail us as at sales@savasbeatie.com, or visit our website at www.savasbeatie.com for additional information.

To my mother

Table of Contents

List of Maps

Maps by Hal Jespersen

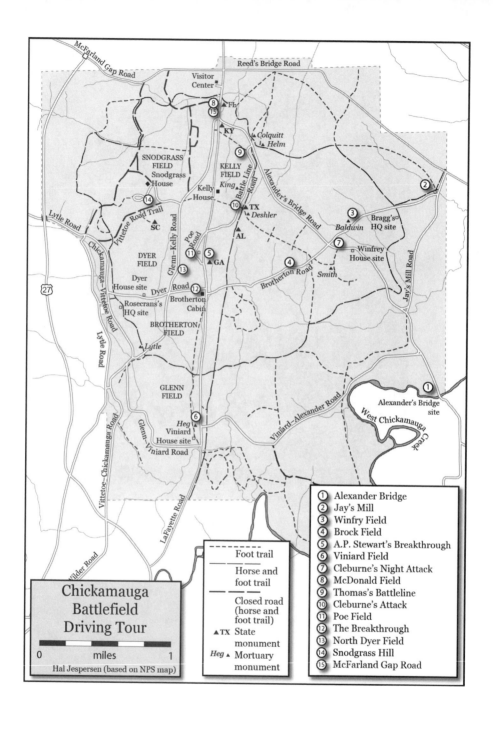

Chickamauga
Battlefield
Driving Tour

0   miles   1

Hal Jespersen (based on NPS map)

---- Foot trail

—— Horse and
foot trail

—— Closed road
(horse and
foot trail)

▲TX State
monument

Heg ▲ Mortuary
monument

① Alexander Bridge
② Jay's Mill
③ Winfry Field
④ Brock Field
⑤ A.P. Stewart's Breakthrough
⑥ Viniard Field
⑦ Cleburne's Night Attack
⑧ McDonald Field
⑨ Thomas's Battleline
⑩ Cleburne's Attack
⑪ Poe Field
⑫ The Breakthrough
⑬ North Dyer Field
⑭ Snodgrass Hill
⑮ McFarland Gap Road

Touring the Battlefield

To give you a comprehensive look at the battlefield, this book deviates from the traditional Park Service driving tour, which only covers the events of the final day of the battle. Directions at the end of each chapter will help you follow along.

Keep in mind that some roads are one way, and others may have heavy traffic. Be mindful of the traffic when crossing through busy intersections and performing U-turns. Please follow all speed limits, and park only in designated parking areas.

As you travel across the battlefield, feel free to explore the landscape around each tour stop and take time to read some of the plaques and inscriptions on the monuments.

The Chickamauga battlefield also has more than 50 miles of trails that wind through the woods and across the fields. Hiking the trails provides an excellent opportunity to see many of the battlefield's hidden monuments, tucked away in otherwise-forgotten glens and groves. While hiking, take insect repellent and be conscious of the possibility of ticks. Hikers should also keep an eye out for snakes.

Acknowledgments

I can honestly say that I was born on the Chickamauga battlefield, or at least a part of it where the local hospital sits today and where Dan McCook's brigade clashed with troopers of Bedford Forrest's Cavalry. However, it was my parents, Bill and Hazel White, who took me there many times as a child  to visit the museum and the field. My grandparents, Curtis Lee and Grace White, fueled my interest with tales of my family during the Civil War, including my grandpa's father hearing the battle at nearby Villanow when he was a boy. I grew up being that boy William Faulkner wrote about, except it wasn't always Gettysburg that fueled my imagination. My Aunt Elaine also contributed a lot to this, carrying me to living history programs and events at Chickamauga and many other Civil War sites when Mom and Dad couldn't. She also bought me my first book on Chickamauga. To them all I owe a special debt. A thanks also to the following teachers who also encouraged and helped foster my love of history: Vicki Crews, Jim Crews, Joella Hood McGill, and Sherman Gibbs. It was a bit of destiny that finally brought me to work at Chickamauga 20 years ago as a living historian and then 13 years ago to work as a ranger.

At Chickamauga and Chattanooga National Military Park (CHCH), I thank my friends and colleagues both past and present. Park Historian Jim Ogden has always been there to answer my questions and encourage me in my endeavors to dig out more details of so many different aspects of the battle.

Among my fellow Chickamauga battlefield explorers and historians, I would like to thank Dave Powell, Dr. Glenn Robertson, Dr. Keith Bohannon, and Robert Carter. Much thanks to Dave, my fellow Chickamauga writer and historian, for his encouragement, for sharing research, and for all the miles we have tramped over the battlefield. Dr. Robertson is the dean of Chickamauga, his research and willingness to challenge the standard view of the battle has greatly benefited students of the battle. Robert is sort of the new kid on the block with his recent guide to the fighting on Snodgrass Hill, but his commitment to helping figure out the fighting there and in other phases of the

All historical photographs courtesy of Chickamauga and Chattanooga National Military Park, except Moxley Sorrel on pg. 148, courtesy of Warner, *Generals in Gray*.

Modern battlefield photography by Chris Mackowski, except on pgs. viii, xi, 6, 7, 12, 13, 31, 33, 59, 106, 123, 125, 132, 138, 154, and 157, courtesy of Lee White; photos of the author on pgs. 159 & 162 from author's personal collection.

battle have helped expand the story in new directions. My good friend Keith Bohannon has helped me in too many ways to list here; I owe him a very special debt.

At Savas Beatie, thank you to Theodore P. Savas for giving me the opportunity to write about an engagement that, ironically, I never thought of writing about. Thank you, too, to his staff for all their support in making this book possible.

At *Emerging Civil War*, thank you to my fellow authors Chris Mackowski and Kris White for helping me with editing, suggestions, and encouragement.

Finally, thank you to Nikki Ellis for her encouragement, threats, and help in getting me back on track while writing this. To my favorite band, the Birthday Massacre, for the soundtrack that helped me break writers block and inspired me to write on. I would also like to thank Brianna Powell, Chuck Dunn, Joe Blunt, Traci and Allen Hyatt, Warren Dickenson, Marshall Burnett, Chris Young, Patrick Lewis, Jeff Hodnett, Lindsey Brown, Ben Wolk, Kristen McClelland, Kim Timmerman, Diane Logan, Charlie Runion, Rick Manion, Preston Brown, and Caroline Lewis, whose strength in adversity is truly inspiring.

For the Emerging Civil War Series

Theodore Savas, publisher
Chris Mackowski, series editor
Kristopher D. White, historical content editor
Sarah Keeney, editorial consultant

Maps by Hal Jespersen
Design and layout by Chris Mackowski

Special thanks to Sarah Keeney, Savas Beatie's marketing director, who has taken a leading role in helping us bring the ECW Series to fruition, and in shaping and editing the design of the books.

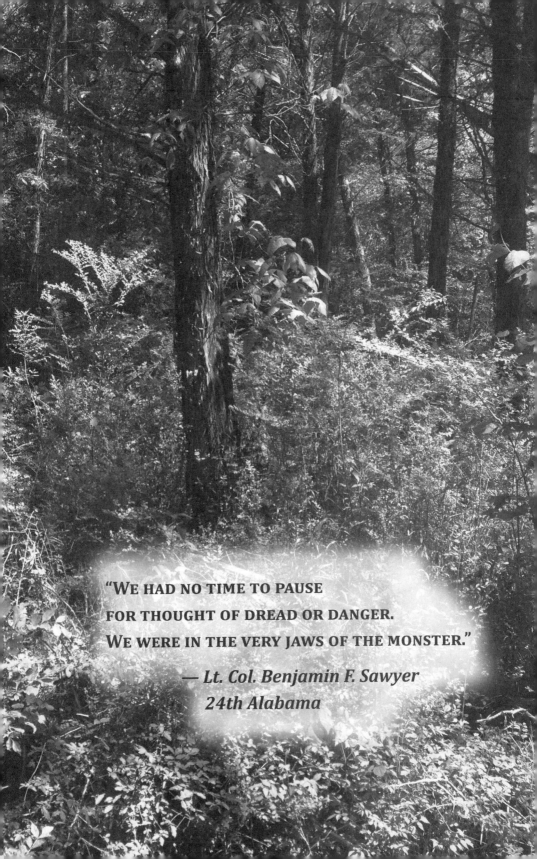

"WE HAD NO TIME TO PAUSE
FOR THOUGHT OF DREAD OR DANGER.
WE WERE IN THE VERY JAWS OF THE MONSTER."

— *Lt. Col. Benjamin F. Sawyer*
24th Alabama

Prologue

"Bushwhacking on a grand scale"—that's how Union Brig. Gen. John Turchin later described the battle of Chickamauga, a brutal engagement in the old-growth timbered forest of northwest Georgia. In the darkened woods, fields, and glades, commanders on both sides sometimes lost sight of the enemy and even their own men as the smoke gathered into a thick deadly fog that made it impossible for generals to command effectively, turning the engagement into what many called "a soldier's fight." The chaos forced men on both sides to act the role of "the captain, the general, and the grand private" all in one, Turchin attested.

"The greatest hero during those long, anxious hours was the soldier," he said.

* * *

Smoke from small brush fires mingled with the black powder smoke of thousands of muskets blending to produce an acrid fog along the slopes of Horseshoe Ridge, making the forest appear even darker than it was. Twilight slowly crawled over the bloody Chickamauga battlefield. Wearily straining his burning eyes to see through the thick smoke, Henry Haynie of the 19th Illinois Infantry noted, "Wasn't death near enough for already? Wasn't there never to be any let up to this thing?"

Whatever respite there was didn't last long. "No time for thinking now," Haynie wrote. "Get to work! And we knelt to fire. Then a forward spring toward our cannon. Boom! Boom! Here; boom, boom! Yonder-both sides firing at point blank range. Jets of blazing powder jump down and scorch the earth round about. Look at those yelling Rebs—how they keep coming on! There's more than a million of them, if there's a hundred! Every man is by now a perfect machine. Him not to think, but to obey, to cling to his gun and aim low. Bullets splash red mud, the earth had been made more by human blood, into our faces, still we do not wince. Bullets, fragments of shell,

The monument for the 125th Ohio, known as "Opdycke's Tigers" in honor of their commander, sits on Snodgrass Hill, where Federals put up a desperate final defense.

Union Brig. Gen. John Turchin called the battle of Chickamauga "the most arduous, the most complicated, and the bloodiest campaign in the West."

grape, and canister sing over and around, louder than songs of Southern katydids, but no one dodges. What's the use? There goes a comrade down—and another! See that fellow keel over as he aims! And the cannoneers—why, there's hardly enough of them left to fire the guns still standing! The ground shakes and trembles, the roar shuts out all sounds from other parts of the line, if there is any left of it."

Haynie and his comrades were standing like oaks as wave after wave of Confederates broke against their defenses. After three days of desperate fighting, it now seemed that at any moment they would be overwhelmed, swallowed whole by the gray horde; however, the Federals managed to hold. Finally, nearing dusk they received the sweet whispered order to fall back and begin the withdrawal. They moved back and made their way northward, toward Chattanooga, as darkness settled over the field.

Thus ended the battle of Chickamauga. After three days of brutal combat, more than 34,000 men had been killed, wounded, or captured, giving the fight the grim distinction of being the second-bloodiest battle of the American Civil War, surpassed only by Gettysburg's bloody butcher's bill. Turchin called it "the most arduous, the most complicated, and the bloodiest campaign in the West . . . ."

The wooded slopes of Snodgrass Hill

Looking over the field in the aftermath of the battle, a young Louisianan, R. L. Lafitte, was shocked. "I saw

the awfullest sight that I ever saw in my life in this battle," he wrote. "The men were piled up on top of one another for miles," he recalled. "The ground was covered with them like leaves . . . ."

Chickamauga is also notable for being the only battle that the Confederacy's ill-starred Army of Tennessee ever won, although the victory would ultimately prove fruitless. They fought the battle for control of the city of Chattanooga—ironically, a city they failed to hold at the end of the battle. It would take more than two months of siege, and five more battles, to ultimately decide the fate of the city.

Monument for the 19th Illinois (above, left)

Lt. Col. Alexander Raffen of the 19th Illinois (top)

* * *

In the years after the war, Lt. Col. Alexander Raffen of the 19th Illinois Infantry visited the battlefield with several other officers of his regiment. "[W]e took a special interest in the parts where our regiment fought[.] the trees in some places are cut down so much by Artillery that it looks as if a tornado had swept over the field, all the trees and stumps are pluged all over with bullits[.] it is astonishing to think that any one could have come off safe without being hit. At the place where we made the last stand the ground is covered with cartridge papers which in itself shows how desperate the struggle must have been."

The Campaign

CHAPTER ONE

SUMMER 1863

"Chattanooga is ours without a struggle, and East Tennessee is free," telegraphed Union Maj. Gen. William Starke Rosecrans to General-in-Chief Henry Halleck on September 9, 1863. After a campaign of deception and maneuver that had forced the Confederate Army of Tennessee to abandon the city, Union troops raised the flag over Chattanooga with hardly a shot fired.

The city's capture was crucial. Chattanooga was considered the gateway to the important industrial heartland of the Confederacy in central Georgia. President Lincoln once said the city was as important as Richmond. Although small, having around 2,500 inhabitants in 1860, Chattanooga had four major rail lines connecting in the vicinity, making it a crucial link in the Confederacy's precarious supply lines. Union armies had tried twice in 1862 to take the town, but failed, enabling the Confederates to use the town as a springboard for an invasion into Kentucky in the fall of '62. Now the Union army sat on the city's doorstep.

Rosecrans, or "Old Rosey" as he was known to the soldiers of his Army of the Cumberland, was a man possessing great talents. He was highly intelligent, creative, and energetic, but he could also be sarcastic, nervous, excitable, stubborn, and hypercritical of both his own officers and his superiors. Born in Ohio on September 6, 1819, Rosecrans attended West Point, graduating fifth in the class of 1842, but being unable to find promotion in the "Old Army," he had resigned and worked as a businessman in the blossoming petroleum business. He was also an inventor, and his dabbling had resulted in an explosion that had severely burned his lower face, forcing him to grow a beard to cover the scars. A devout Roman Catholic and War Democrat, he had made many close friends, but also quite a few bitter enemies.

Taking Chattanooga was Rosecrans's destiny from

The city of Chattanooga, as seen today from Point Park at the top of Lookout Mountain

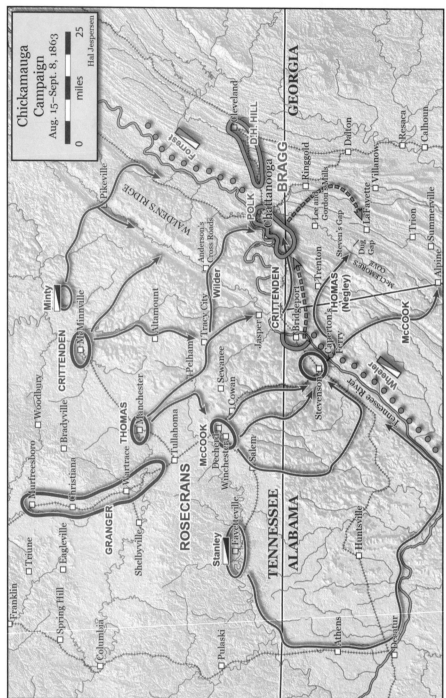

CHICKAMAUGA CAMPAIGN—Realizing that a head-on assault against Chattanooga would be a disaster, Rosecrans devised a campaign of deception and maneuver. Rosecrans ordered a force into the hills and ridges north of Chattanooga to make a lot of noise, distracting Bragg from the real Federal move: a dangerous gamble that split the Army of the Cumberland and moved it through the difficult terrain below Chattanooga with the goal of striking toward Bragg's supply line from Atlanta in the hopes of forcing Confederates to abandon Chattanooga and retreat to Atlanta.

Union commander
Maj. Gen. William C.
Rosecrans (left) and
Confederate commander
Gen. Braxton Bragg (right)

the day he took command of his army in late October of 1862. "The great objects to be kept in view in your operations in the field," read his first orders, "are: First, to drive the enemy from Kentucky and Middle Tennessee; second, to take and hold East Tennessee, cutting the line of railroad at Chattanooga, Cleveland, or Athens, so as to destroy the connection of the valley of Virginia with Georgia and the other Southern States."

By late August of 1863, Rosecrans was moving to finish this directive. All that stood in his way was the Army of Tennessee and its dour commander, Gen. Braxton Bragg.

Like Rosecrans, Bragg was rather eccentric. Both were men of great talent, and both had made powerful enemies. Bragg, however, did not enjoy the success that Rosecrans had. Born in North Carolina in 1817, Bragg attended West Point, graduating fifth in the class of 1837. He went on to serve in the Second Seminole War, and then became a hero in the War with Mexico by saving Zachary Taylor's army at the battle of Buena Vista. While in the army, Bragg developed a reputation as a whistleblower, a strict disciplinarian, and a man unafraid of clashing with men of great power, having several go-rounds with Gen. Winfield Scott. He finally resigned from the army after a quarrel with Secretary of War Jefferson Davis. When Davis became president of the Confederacy, Bragg despaired of being given any meaningful role due to his fight with Davis, but all was forgotten, and Bragg rose rapidly through the general ranks, taking command of his army in the summer of 1862 with high expectations.

A year later, Bragg looked to have aged a decade. He seemed to be battling some of his subordinates more than the Union army, and although he had saved Chattanooga from capture in 1862, he was now in danger of losing it.

Rosecrans had first clashed with Bragg on the last day of 1862 in the battle of Stones River, a meeting that Bragg had nearly won but for Rosecrans's stubborn nature.

Lt. Gen. Daniel Harvey Hill
was welcomed into the Army
of Tennessee by Bragg, but
quickly their relationship
soured as Hill delivered
excuses instead of action.

Maj. Gen. Thomas C. Hindman

After the Confederate defeat, Bragg retreated into the breadbasket area of Middle Tennessee, establishing his army in the area around Tullahoma to block Rosecrans. In late June of 1863, Rosecrans moved against Bragg in a nearly bloodless campaign that proved disastrous for the Army of Tennessee and cost the Confederacy a critical source of corn and wheat. Bragg retreated out of Middle Tennessee to Chattanooga with Rosecrans pursuing to the western base of the Cumberland Plateau. Bragg began to plead for reinforcements.

Over the subsequent weeks, Rosecrans built up supplies and planned his next move. Bragg's army, meanwhile, slowly began to grow. He gained greater control of Eastern Tennessee and the forces there under Maj. Gen. Simon Buckner, and he enjoyed the return of Maj. Gen. John Breckinridge's division, which had been sent to Mississippi just prior to the opening of the Tullahoma Campaign. Word even circulated that he would get men from Robert E. Lee's fabled Army of Northern Virginia.

Bragg also received support with the arrival of several new officers, notably Maj. Gen. Thomas C. Hindman, a general whose aggressive nature had earned him the nickname "Lion of the South," and acting Lt. Gen. Daniel Harvey Hill. Technically, Hill was a major general, but he was in the process of being promoted; the Confederate Congress just needed to vote on his confirmation. Hill had commanded one of Lee's better divisions, but his acerbic tongue and sour personality had caused him to be promoted out of that army.

Hill arrived in the West to take command of Lt. Gen. William J. Hardee's Corps following Hardee's transfer to Mississippi. Hill's troops, along with the troops of veteran commander Lt. Gen. Leonidas Polk, made up the backbone of the Army of Tennessee as reinforcements began to arrive.

Polk, known as "the Fighting Bishop," was a West Point graduate who also served as the bishop of the Episcopal diocese of Louisiana. Early in the war, he served in various positions in the western theater, and by mid-1862, he found himself serving under Bragg. Trouble between the two started almost immediately and flared up following the autumn campaign into Perryville, Kentucky, when Polk began an ongoing effort to have Bragg ousted. Confederate President Jefferson Davis refused to intervene, though, and the sour atmosphere between the two generals festered. With Hill's addition to his army, Bragg now had two of the Confederacy's most prickly subordinates to contend with— not just the Army of the Cumberland.

* * *

Rosecrans realized that a head-on move against Chattanooga would be disastrous and doomed to fail, so he once again decided to use deception and maneuver. He waited until the corn crop was coming in—which would allow him to take advantage of the fresh crop and not overtax his already-overburdened supply lines— then launched his move against Chattanooga in the final days of August, sending a diversionary force into the hills and ridges north of the city to make a lot of noise and feign against the Tennessee River there. These men dragged limbs behind horses to stir up huge clouds of dust and built multiple campfires to make it seem that tens of thousands of troops were moving. They chopped down trees and banged on barrels to make it sound like they were constructing pontoon bridges, and an artillery battery even shelled Chattanooga from the north side.

Lt. Gen. Leonidas Polk was the Army of Tennessee's senior corps commander. Polk, the pre-war bishop of the southwest, owned several sugarcane plantations and was the largest slaveholder in the army. He was also a cousin of President James K. Polk.

The ruse worked. Bragg became convinced that Federals intended to cross the Tennessee River to the north of Chattanooga and shifted the bulk of his army in that direction. Meanwhile, Rosecrans shifted the rest of his army over the Cumberland Mountains and moved them toward the Tennessee River in the vicinity of the railroad towns of Stevenson and Bridgeport, Alabama, south and west of Chattanooga. There, Rosecrans split his army into three columns consisting mainly of a corps a piece.

The XXI Corps, under Maj. Gen. Thomas Leonidas Crittenden, would move directly toward Chattanooga. Crittenden was a capable general with strong political connections due to the influence of his father, Kentucky Sen. John Crittenden.

The XIV Corps, under Maj. Gen. George Henry Thomas, would move into the rear of the Confederates to make a stab at the Western and Atlantic Railroad, Bragg's lifeline to Atlanta. Thomas, Rosecrans's most capable and dependable subordinate, was a Virginia native who had remained loyal to the Union at the expense of being disowned by his family.

Lt. Gen. James Longstreet led a detachment of veterans from Robert E. Lee's Army of Northern Virginia, sent west as reinforcements.

The final column consisted of the XX Corps and the army's cavalry under the overall command of the XX Corps commander, Maj. Gen. Alexander McDowell McCook. McCook's objective was to move even further to the south and make for the city of Rome, an important industrial center along a route toward Atlanta. The youngest corps commander in U.S. service and a member of Ohio's "Fighting McCooks," McCook was an 1852 West Point graduate, but a fellow officer described him as a "chucklehead."

The cavalry, meanwhile, was commanded by Brig. Gen. David Sloan Stanley; however, ill health soon forced Stanley from the field, and he was replaced by Brig. Gen.

Robert S. Mitchell. The army's Reserve Corps, under the aggressive Gordon Granger, would continue to guard the army's ever-extending supply lines.

Rosecrans calculated that one of two things would happen: Bragg would remain in Chattanooga, fixated on the Federal deception, and be trapped with his supply lines cut; or, Bragg would learn about the move into his rear, abandon Chattanooga, and retreat to Atlanta. Either one would be a victory for Rosecrans. It was a bold but dangerous plan that could net him either a great victory or annihilation.

The mountainous terrain around Chattanooga proved to be a formidable obstacle for the Union Army to overcome. Sgt. William Miller of the 75th Indiana noted, "This is the roughest place we have found yet. The pass is narrow and coal mines all around us. On one side it is perpendicular hundreds of feet high and on the other is the valley hundreds of feet below with only a narrow road up the mountain. If the Rebels can't hold such passes as this what can they defend?"

Rosecrans's men began moving out from their bivouacs on August 29, crossing the Tennessee at several locations with little or no opposition. They then began crossing first the 2,000-foot-high Sand Mountain and then the 2,200-foot Lookout Mountain. "The weather was delightful," remembered Lt. Albion Tourgee of the 105th Ohio, "the autumnal brown of the oaks being relieved by the gold of the hickories that grew upon the slopes and the softer tints of the chestnuts upon the level plateaus which constituted the summit. The roads leading eastward were little used—hardly more than cross country trails. There were heavy details for pioneer work, but even artillery and wagons had to be held by ropes to prevent them from falling off the steep roadways, while the teams were doubled at the worst points, making slow work. The night fell long before we reached the summit, and all night long, with torches and ropes, and shouts and jests, we dragged the lumbering wagons up the sharp incline."

A gunner in the 11th Indiana Battery, some 20 miles south, noted, "This mountain march cost us several good horses; the heat and dust was, to say the least, terrible and water very scarce." Another wrote:

> *This mountain was so difficult to surmount that an entire platoon of men and six horses were required to bring up a piece, and to enliven the effort a band would play 'Bony Crossing the Alps.' We found red cedar in abundance, likewise gooseberries, saw no blackberries as in the valley, found peaches in a wild state even growing on the overhanging crags. The vegetation and foliage generally was much different and more attractive, and the atmosphere was fine. Occasionally we would pass . . . a cabin built of logs containing to us a simple, honest, but outlandish looking*

people, who greeted us in a friendly way…we found deserted homes which had been raided by rebel guerillas, the loyal inhabitants having become 'refugees.'

Through all of this, Bragg remained unaware of the threat in his rear. His cavalry, the eyes and ears of his army, simply failed him. Bragg only learned of the presence of Union troops in his rear on September 7 from several citizens who had recently been visited by the Union army. Bragg ordered the evacuation of Chattanooga and a march southward into Georgia and the town of LaFayette. Wheeler's Cavalry Corps was ordered up to find and delay the Union advance.

After Bragg evacuated the city, Crittenden moved in and took control, sending word of the bloodless capture to Rosecrans. Rosecrans was emboldened to the point of recklessness, calling Thomas to meet with him and plan a pursuit of the Confederates. Thomas advised against pursuit, though, instead suggesting that they should consolidate their forces in Chattanooga before leaping into another campaign. Rosecrans had become overconfident, though, and disregarded Thomas's advice. He sent orders to Crittenden to push southward while Thomas moved on LaFayette to try to incept Bragg.

Little did Rosecrans know that Bragg had stopped running. Bragg had finally learned of the Army of the Cumberland's positions and realized he had a golden opportunity to destroy each column in detail.

Bragg ordered Hill to block the Union advance on LaFayette in McClemore's Cove, a box shaped canyon a few miles west of the town, with while Maj. Gen. Thomas Hindman's division of Polk's Corps would attack southward into the mouth of the cove and hit the Union troops in the flank. The attack could be devastating.

In McClemore's Cove, Union Brig. Gen. James Negley's division, leading Thomas's Corps, slowly made its way forward into Bragg's trap. However, when the time came to spring it, nothing happened. Hill had found fault with the plan: "I believed that the intended junction would be impossible," he contended, "and certainly no surprise could be effected." "The Lion," Hindman, meanwhile, had turned into a kitten and refused to attack, fearing he was outnumbered.

Negley soon realized the danger he was in, and

In McClemore's Cove, Bragg hoped to destroy part of George Thomas' XIV Corps, but the failure of two of his subordinates to follow his orders resulted in a missed opportunity that would haunt the army in the days that followed.

As Rosecrans raced to pull his army back together, the Lee's and Gordon's Mills became the concentration point for the army as Bragg tried to bring it to battle.

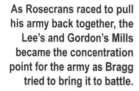

Lee's and Gordon's Mills today

before Bragg could get his forces moving, it was too late. Negley and the division following him made their way back to the safety of Lookout Mountain. Bragg's golden opportunity dissolved into dust. "The whole affair proved a miserable failure," lamented one Confederate officer.

Rosecrans now became aware of the great danger he was in and immediately sent out orders for McCook to abandon his march and unite with Thomas, and then together they would move to join Crittenden, who was halted at Lee's and Gordon's Mills along the banks of Chickamauga Creek. Now a race began, with Bragg looking for an opportunity to strike Rosecrans before the Union commander could pull all of his forces back together. Rosecrans saddled his men northward using Chickamauga Creek as a shield, leapfrogging units from one defensive position to another. Rosecrans rode into the community of Crawfish Springs, a short distance to the rear of Crittenden's position, and established his headquarters at the Gordon Lee mansion.

Bragg saw that he had one more chance to strike Rosecrans a fatal blow before the Army of the Cumberland was reunited.

At the Visitor Center

The battle of Chickamauga is largely remembered for the actions of September 20, the final day of the bloody engagement, but the battle consisted of much more. To truly understand it, we will follow the course of events as they happened across the dark and bloody woodlands.

The battlefield visitor center

Before you tour the battlefield, you may wish to go to the visitor center. An excellent orientation film and exhibits on the campaign and battle will give you a good overview of the places and stories that you are about to see and read about. Restrooms are available.

Outside the visitor center, note the cannon

display. In the forest, where artillerists had difficulty maneuvering and aiming their pieces, these weapons proved more of a hindrance than asset. However, in the open fields around the visitor center, artillery made its presence felt. Early on September 20, Union artillerists, members of Capt. Lyman Bridge's Illinois Battery, put up a gallant—if ultimately futile—effort to slow Confederate attacks in the area. Later the famed 5th Company of the Washington Artillery would occupy this ground and then move south in support of the Confederate advance. They would fire an astonishing 682 rounds in only three hours from their six guns into the woods and fields to the south. In the final hours of the battle, Confederate artillery again occupied this ground only to be driven off by a desperate Union effort. You can see the final gun position behind the visitor center.

→ TO STOP 1

From the visitor center parking lot, turn right onto the LaFayette Road and make your way .22 miles to the intersection with Alexander's Bridge Road. Turn right. Follow Alexander's Bridge Road 2.6 miles to the parking spaces adjacent to the modern Alexander Bridge.

GPS: N 34.90722 W 85.22984

The cannon display outside the visitor center presents the various types of cannons both armies used during the battle.

Cannon behind the visitor center mark the spot where Confederate artillerists set up on September 20.

Across the street from the visitor center, a monument to the 42nd Indiana marks the spot where the Hoosiers made a stand against Confederates on September 20 before being overrun.

The Gordon Lee Mansion, built in 1847 for James Gordon, overlooks Crawfish Springs. In the days before Chickamauga, the home served as the headquarters for General Rosecrans; during the battle, it was a major Union field hospital, and it witnessed some of the final fighting by Wheeler's cavalry. The mansion is operated today by the city of Chickamauga, where visitors can walk the grounds and view several surviving outbuildings, including former slave quarters.

Alexander's Bridge

CHAPTER TWO

SEPTEMBER 18, 1863

General Thomas Crittenden's Corps held a strong position on the high ground overlooking a bridge at the Lee's and Gordon's Mills. "[W]orks were thrown up along the banks of the stream, and the position became tolerably secure," a member of the 64th Ohio noted. Miles away, Rosecrans slowly leapfrogged the rest of the army in Crittenden's direction.

Bragg was not idle, either, and plotted to destroy Rosecrans's army before the Federal consolidation happened. Bragg formulated a new plan to strike the Union left flank with most of his army by crossing the Chickamauga Creek north of Crittenden and then sweeping down like a massive tidal wave, cutting Rosecrans off from Chattanooga and pushing the Union army back into McClemore's Cove and crushing it against the mountains. "Your generals will lead you; you have but to respond to assure us a glorious triumph over an insolent foe. I know what your response will be," Bragg confidently announced to his army. "Trusting in God and the justice of our cause, and nerved by the love of the dear ones at home, failure is impossible and victory must be ours."

Rosecrans seemed to sense the growing danger to his northern flank. Meeting with Col. John T. Wilder, commander of the famed "Lightning Brigade" at his headquarters in the luxurious mansion of James Gordon in Crawfish Springs, Rosecrans gave orders for Wilder to proceed north beyond Crittenden's left flank. There, Wilder would assist Scottish-born Col. Robert Minty's cavalry brigade in screening the crossings of the Chickamauga. He'd do that by deploying his men to defend Alexander's Bridge, a point halfway between Lee's and Gordon's Mills and Minty's cavalry videttes, deployed east of the creek covering the approaches to Reed's Bridge.

Being mounted infantry, Wilder's command was

Federals hunkered along the banks of Chickamauga Creek to resist Confederate attempts to cross at Alexander's Bridge.

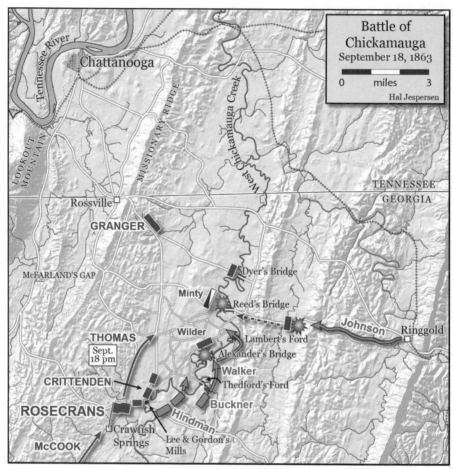

SEPTEMBER 18, 1863—Bragg's plan called for a three-pronged move around the northern flank of the Union forces to cross the Chickamauga Creek, cut the routes into Chattanooga, and launch a crushing blow against the Union XXI Corps at Lee's and Gordon's Mills. Things fell apart as Bushrod Johnson's column ran into Robert Minty's Union cavalrymen, while Walker's column ran into part of Wilder's Brigade at Alexander's Bridge. Buckner, hearing the other fights, decided to wait until a clearer picture developed before crossing the Chickamauga.

A Spencer repeating rifle, on display at the battlefield visitor center. With seven shots, the Spencer gave the men of the Lightning Brigade a distinct edge over their opponents, who were armed with single-shot muzzle loaders.

perfect for this assignment. The men could be quickly moved about like cavalry, but dismounted to fight on foot like infantry. However, what truly gave them an edge was their armament: Spencer repeating rifles. The Spencer was a leaver-action rifle able to hold seven shots that could be fired in quick succession before having to be reloaded.

Wilder's troopers arrived on the Alexander property on the evening of September 17 and went into camp.

*   *   *

From its source in McClemore's Cove, the Chickamauga Creek wound its way north into the Tennessee River near Chattanooga. The creek created a natural barrier, being 80 to 100 feet wide, deep in places,

The sluggish Chickamauga proved to be a formidable barrier between the two armies in the days leading up to the battle—deep and with high banks, only crossable at a few bridges and fords.

and with high banks that made it impossible to easily cross except at a few fords and bridges.

John P. Alexander, a prosperous farmer, purchased a farm in 1859 that bordered the creek at one of the bridges. The bridge, a broken-down wooden structure with flooring made of planks and old fence rails, soon bore Alexander's name. His farm covered 120 acres on either side of the Alexander Bridge Road, with the house situated on a rise about half a mile back from the bridge. Alexander brought his family and his 35 slaves to the farm, becoming the second-largest slave owner in the area. Alexander set about farming the land, planting a peach orchard near his home and cultivating his fields in corn and oats. However, trouble quickly came to Alexander: he murdered a man and, fleeing prosecution, moved to Tennessee, leaving his farm behind. In his absence, an arrangement was evidently made for James Lee—a prominent local businessman, co-owner of Lee's and Gordon's Mills, and closet Unionist—to manage the farm. It was in his care when Wilder's men arrived.

Wilder deployed his command in the fields around the Alexander house and in the fields bordering the Alexander Bridge Road. Captain Eli Lilly's 18th Indiana Battery deployed his battery of three-inch ordinance rifles adjacent to the house while the mounted infantry deployed in the open fields between there and the creek. Before all daylight was lost, Wilder climbed into a tree in

In the yard of the Alexander house, Capt. Eli Lilly's 18th Indiana Battery provided support for the mounted infantry defending Alexander's Bridge.

The fight for Reed's Bridge began the bloody three days that are known as the battle of Chickamauga.

A monument to the 7th Pennsylvania Cavalry features one of the park's many bas relief bronze tablets. A private from the unit fired the first shot of the battle.

the yard of the house and surveyed the surrounding area, noticing an ominous cloud of dust billowing up from the southeast. "That is the advance of Bragg's army," he said to Lilly and his officers.

Bragg's plan was to cross the Chickamauga at four points. His columns would then converge to launch his planned flank attack. Brigadier General Bushrod Rust Johnson would lead a division to cross at Reed's Bridge. Major General William Henry Talbot "Shot Pouch" Walker's Reserve Corps would take Alexander's Bridge, while Gen. Simon Bolivar Buckner's Corps crossed at Thedford's and Dalton's Fords. General Thomas Hindman's division would demonstrate against Lee's and Gordon's Mills.

Early in the morning of September 18, Bragg set things in motion, but trouble quickly developed as Johnson's men cautiously began to make their way across Peavine Creek. Private Samuel Walters of the 7th Pennsylvania Cavalry raised his Smith Carbine, took aim at a distant figure, and fired.

The battle of Chickamauga began.

Troopers of Irish-born Col. Robert Minty's cavalry brigade, fighting dismounted, opened fire at Johnson's column, which began to deploy for battle. As Johnson's men began to advance, Minty's men ran back to their horses and mounted up and rode back to another position to fight. With less than a thousand cavalrymen, Minty faced overwhelming odds; he was outnumbered by more than five to one. Still, he remained determined to do everything possible to delay the Confederate advance.

Minty's resistance stopped Johnson's march, forcing him to deploy his men from their marching column into line of battle all the while being peppered by the gunfire of Minty's men. Just as Confederates began to advance, the cavalrymen mounted their horses and fell back to another position where the whole process was repeated again. In this manner, Minty slowed the Confederate advance to a crawl. It was late in the afternoon before

Johnson finally came in sight of Reed's Bridge.

As the sound of combat drifted southward, Wilder received a plea from Minty for assistance and ordered most of two regiments, the 72nd Indiana and 123rd Illinois, to move to the north to help the beleaguered cavalrymen. This left him with the 17th Indiana, five companies of the 98th Illinois, three companies of the 72nd Indiana and four rifled guns of Lilly's battery—in all, less than a thousand men to defend Alexander's Bridge.

The first sign of trouble came when a group of Hoosiers foraging for food on the east side of the creek stumbled into a Confederate cavalry patrol. The Federals raced back across Alexander's bridge with the cavalrymen close behind, but a few well-directed shots soon convinced them to give up their chase and make a hasty retreat out of the range of Wilder's deadly Spencers. About noon, Walker's infantry approached to make his crossing and, detecting Wilder's presence, ordered an assault to take the bridge. That unfortunate task fell to the Mississippi brigade of Brig. Gen. Edward Walthall. Ironically one year and a day earlier, Walthall, then the colonel of 29th Mississippi, had fought Wilder at Munfordville, Kentucky, where Wilder was forced to surrender. Now Wilder would have some revenge.

Under the eye of his division commander, Brig. Gen. St. John Liddell, Walthall formed his men for the assault, deploying along the east side of the road with the left brigade, the 34th Mississippi, resting on the Alexander Bridge Road. As support, Liddell ordered Col. Daniel Govan's Arkansas brigade and his artillery to deploy on the west side of the road. Skirmishers were deployed, and then bugles called the advance.

Walthall's Mississippians surged forward, but things seemed to unravel immediately. The route of the attack was through very broken terrain and a thick patch of woods, which caused the right of the brigade to lose their alignment as they struggled to make their way through honeysuckle vines and black berry bushes. Meanwhile, the rest of the brigade drifted westward with the center of the brigade, the 29th Mississippi, coming to advance down the road. They emerged from the woods and into an old field about 350 yards from the bridge. Watching from Alexander's Bridge, Sgt. James Barnes of the 72nd Indiana watched the scene develop before him, and despite the broken alignment, he was impressed. "They came up in splendid style, lines well dressed, step firm, even and steady, bayonets fixed and gleaming in the sun," he wrote.

The inspiring scene was soon interrupted as Lilly's guns opened fire, hurling shells into the Mississippians.

Col. John T. Wilder commanded the "Lightning Brigade." A native of New York who relocated to Indiana, Wilder saw the value of speed and firepower and successfully campaigned to get his infantry command mounted and armed with repeating rifles. The troopers of the Lightning Brigade clung to their branch of service—infantry—even though on horseback, going as far as to remove the distinctive yellow trim from their jackets when issued cavalry uniforms.

Col. Robert Minty's command was known as the "Saber Brigade" and fought a successful delaying action that slowed the Confederate advance on Reed's Bridge to a painful crawl.

Maj. Gen. Bushrod Johnson

Brig. Gen. St. John Liddell

One of the markers denoting the location of Wilder's line sits in the trees near Alexander's Bridge.

Confederate artillery responded in kind, but it was outmatched in this long-range contest.

As Walthall's men neared the creek, Wilder's troops opened fire. The Mississippi line melted away under a leaden hail. They reformed to try their luck once more but met similar results. Hearing this gunfire, Buckner's advance across the creek at Thedford's and Dalton's Fords, a short distance to the south, came to a halt, moving only to secure the crossing and waiting to see further developments.

Walthall realized that his assaults were useless. Wilder's men had ripped the flooring from the bridge and used the planking to construct a small fort in the road on their side of the bridge, blocking the only way across because the creek was "deep, the banks steep and impassible." Learning this, Walker ordered the battered Mississippians to break off. The dejected Confederates now moved to the north to Byram's Ford, which was unguarded, and began to cross the creek there.

*   *   *

While Wilder fought his battle for Alexander's Bridge, Minty struggled to defend Reed's Bridge. Despite their stubborn defense, though, the Federals were unable to hold and were forced to retreat. By the late afternoon, Johnson's Confederates finally moved across the Chickamauga. Minty fell back westward toward the LaFayette Road and sent word to Wilder that his left flank was now in danger.

Wilder, in turn, ordered his men to extricate themselves and move down the Alexander Road, still guarding Crittenden's flank. Wilder's stand cost him a handful of men killed and wounded, but it inflicted more than 100 casualties among Walthall's troops and, most importantly, bought critical time. Even though the Confederates were now across the sluggish Chickamauga, it was too late for them to launch Bragg's intended attack. Things would have to wait for the next morning.

That evening, not knowing the exact nature of the threat spilling across the creek to his north, Rosecrans ordered George Thomas to move his XIV Corps from its position in the center to the army's left. Thomas's men would have to march all night to come into position along the LaFayette Road in the vicinity of the Kelly farm shortly after dawn. Meanwhile, Bragg ordered his command to finish their crossings and go into position for the attack he expected to make the next morning. He also ordered cavalryman Brig. Gen. Nathan Bedford Forrest to screen the army toward the LaFayette Road—a task

Forrest failed to execute properly when he ordered his troopers to camp on the east side of the Chickamauga.

Forrest's mistake nearly brought disaster for the Confederates the next morning.

At Alexander's Bridge

You are now standing along the banks of the Chickamauga Creek, cutting its way northward to the Tennessee River. At the time of the battle, this area would have been large farm fields, part of the Alexander farm, a pastoral setting that opened one of the bloodiest engagements of the American Civil War. Wilder's stand at Alexander's Bridge heralded a new age in warfare: it was the first major battle in which repeating firearms were used, and it showed that these weapons could even the odds in the face of even overwhelming numbers.

The originial Alexander's Bridge as it looked during the war.

This area, now wooded, was drastically different in 1863: 120 acres of corn and oats with only a strip of woods along the banks of the creek. Walking down to the banks of the Chickamauga will give a good understanding of the obstacle that the terrain presented to the Confederates in September of 1863. Although not a wide stream, the high limestone banks presented an impressive barrier to contend with, and although infantrymen might be able to struggle across, there was no way supply wagons or artillery could do so except at fords or bridges.

The original park commission bridge was relocated to the city of Chickamauga in the Holland-Watson Veterans Memorial Park, where it remains on display.

Two stone markers along the banks mark the positions of Wilder's line here. Wilder's men would have been hunkered down among the trees or behind their bridge plank barricade here as they watched the parade ground advance of Walthall's brigade before opening up upon them with their repeaters. The sound would have been deafening as they fired shot after shot in rapid succession into the shocked Mississippians, stopping their advance cold on the opposite side of the stream and forcing them to look for an alternative place to make their way across.

→ **TO STOP 2**

Alexander's Bridge today.

Return to your vehicle. Turn around and retrace your route back up Alexander's Bridge Road 0.6 miles to Jay's Mill Road. Turn right onto Jay's Mill Road and proceed up the road approximately 0.9 miles until you come to the wayside at Jay's Mill.

GPS: N 34.92895 W 85.22972

Jay's Mill

CHAPTER THREE

SEPTEMBER 19, 1863

The morning of September 19 arrived foggy and cold. The first frost of the year had arrived during the night. The previous evening, Dan McCook's and John Mitchell's brigades of Granger's Reserve Corps arrived along the northwestern edge of the field along the Reed's Bridge Road, having been ordered down from Rossville in response to one of Minty's calls for support earlier in the day. McCook, in the lead, arrived unaware of the large numbers of Confederates in his vicinity.

As he deployed his men, his skirmish line stumbled upon the rear echelon—the band and medical personnel—from Johnson's rear brigade, Brig. Gen. Evander McNair's Arkansasans. McCook came under the notion that only this one brigade had made its way across the creek, even though he'd made contact with a Confederate cavalry skirmish line around midnight. The idea was too tempting for McCook, and he set out to seal the fate of this lone brigade.

To do so, McCook first sent a force to destroy Reed's Bridge, a task attempted by soldiers from the 69th Ohio. The Buckeyes set fire to the bridge, then made a hasty retreat before making sure their deed was done. The bridge failed to burn due to the quick reaction of nearby Confederates and the sloppy arsonists of the 69th.

A short distance in front of McCook's skirmish line was the steam-powered sawmill of William Jay, who had cleared the field that bore his name, and a spring that supplied the water necessary for the boiler that powered the saw. This water source now proved an enticement for some of McCook's thirsty soldiers who made their way there to fill their canteens; others built a small fire and began to boil their morning coffee.

However, the light of their fire flickering in the gloom drew the attention of a small patrol from the 1st Georgia Cavalry who opened fire upon the careless

As Forrest's troopers plunged into the woods west of Jay's Mill, they were stunned by a staggering volley from Col. John Croxton's infantry.

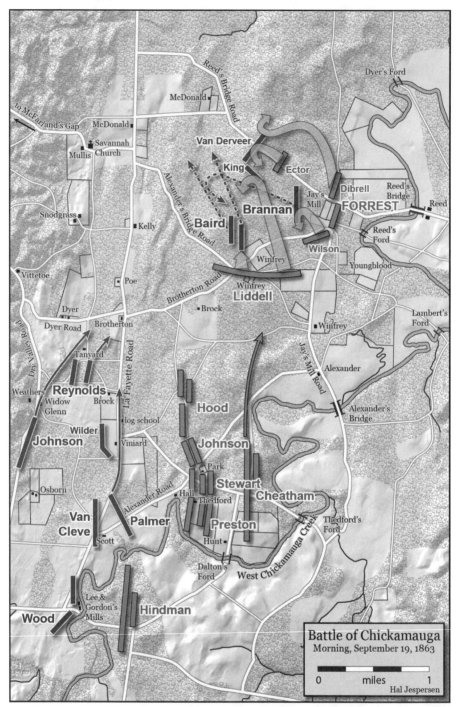

Battle of Chickamauga
Morning, September 19, 1863

0   miles   1

Hal Jespersen

MORNING, SEPTEMBER 19—The battle of Chickamauga continued on the morning of September 19 when it ignited near Jay's Mill. Starting as a small engagement, it steadily grew, spreading to the southwest as both sides rushed troops into the fight in a deadly game of tic-tac-toe. By late morning, fighting had reached the Alexander Bridge Road as more men from both sides were moved toward the sound of the guns.

Union soldiers. Shots were fired in the predawn twilight, drawing the rest of the Georgia regiment forward and sending the startled Union soldiers running back to the safety of their picket line. The Georgians pushed on and soon engaged McCook's pickets who fell back to their main line, which McCook was deploying to face his unexpected visitors. The firing brought the rest of Davidson's brigade into action, and soon the boom of Capt. Gustave Huwald's "Jackass" Battery of Mountain Howitzers—small cannons that were hauled around on muleback and quickly assembled for combat—rent the early morning air.

In the predawn light, both sides began pushing against each other with escalating force.

Just as the firing became general along the line, McCook received an order from Granger to return immediately to Rossville. McCook reluctantly ordered his and Mitchell's brigade to withdraw back up the Reed's Bridge Road. Davidson pursued them a short distance, then returned to the vicinity of Jay's Mill. McCook, meanwhile, sullenly made his way back to the intersection of the LaFayette Road where he discovered Thomas's Corps. McCook left his command and made his way to Thomas to inform him that he had destroyed Reed's Bridge and that one enemy brigade was now trapped by his actions on this side of the creek. McCook then returned to his command and made his way back to Rossville.

The news of the presence of Confederates on the west side of the Chickamauga left Thomas with a tough decision to make. Rosecrans did not want to bring on a general engagement until all of the Army of the Cumberland was reunited, and McCook's Corps had yet to link up with Crittenden. At the same time, however, destroying a lone brigade would be of little risk. Besides, pushing through the forest toward the creek would put Thomas in a better position to protect Crittenden's flank.

Thomas decided to risk it. He ordered Brig. Gen. John Brannan to advance his division from Kelly's field

Brig. Gen. Nathan Bedford Forrest commanded one of two cavalry corps of the Army of Tennessee. Though having a fearsome reputation as a fighter and raider, Forrest struggled with the tasks required of him working within the structure of the army.

The site of Jay's Mill

Maj. Gen. George Henry Thomas commanded the XIV Corps. Thomas's men went forward on the morning of September 19 after having marched all night to arrive in the vicinity of Kelly field.

into the forest to look for the Confederate brigade. Brannan, in turn, ordered Col. John Croxton to lead the way, while Col. Ferdinand Van Derveer's brigade advanced on Croxton's left along the Reed's Bridge Road, and Col. John Connell's brigade followed Van Derveer as the division reserve. Brannan's men were less than thrilled by the bugle calls that announced the orders to fall in, as they had just settled down to sleep or to boil coffee and prepare breakfast. Curses against the generals and the Confederates filled the air as they fell back into ranks.

Back at Jay's Mill, Bedford Forrest joined Davidson, along with division commander Brig. Gen. John Pegram, and decided that he had better determine what lay in the woods to the west. As the rest of the brigade dismounted and began to prepare breakfast, Pegram ordered the 10th Confederate Cavalry to make a mounted reconnaissance toward the LaFayette Road. They had gone a short distance when the morning calm was shattered by a blast of musketry. "One tremendous volley rang along the whole line . . ." noted one of Croxton's men. "[A]ll was smoke, then dust from struggling steeds, a few riderless horses were running here and there save which nothing was seen of that cavalry."

At Jay's Mill the thunderous roar caused many men to leap to their feet and some onto their horses as officers and men tried to determine what was happening. Private J. W. Minnich of the 6th Georgia Cavalry witnessed the scene as the 10th came spilling out of the woods and barreling through the rest of Davidson's brigade. "[T]he demoralized and panic-stricken troopers came down upon us over the crest with a rush that threatened to swamp us . . ." he wrote. "Wild eyed, hatless, horseless, without guns many of them wounded and bleeding, two on one horse, rider less horses by the score, some

Dan McCook's brigade put up stiff resistance against Forrest's cavalry before receiving orders to withdraw back up the Reed's Bridge Road.

frenzied by wounds and pain, some on three legs leaping painfully, men yelling at the top of their voice, 'Git Boys! The woods are full of Yankees.'" The stampede through Davidson's brigade threw everyone into disarray, and many joined the fleeing 10th Confederate, but Forrest, Pegram, and other officers soon had the men back in ranks and moving westward to confront Croxton.

In the woods just beyond the western edge of Jay's field, Davidson's dismounted troopers made contact and opened fire. Croxton brought his whole brigade on line and the woods came alive with whizzing bullets. Forrest seemed to be everywhere, ordering the line to attack, hammering Croxton's line again and again. Despite being outnumbered, the spirited defense ground the Union line to a halt and a static firefight developed. Forrest took this opportunity to call for help from the nearby infantry of Walker's Corps even as he called for the return of his old division, then on assignment to General Polk.

Col. Dan McCook, the younger brother of corps commander Alexander McCook

Bragg received word of the encounter along with Forrest's plea for assistance from Walker. Bragg gave his consent and soon Col. Claudius Wilson's Georgia brigade was making its way north toward the sound of the fighting. Hurrying up the dusty Jay's Mill Road, the Georgians wheeled into line and came into position on the left of Davidson's beleaguered cavalrymen. Forrest's old brigade arrived, too, from its assignment with Polk and moved into line on Davidson's right even as the Georgians pitched forward to strike the flank of Federal line. Howling the Rebel Yell, the Georgians forced Croxton to refuse his left to face the oncoming onslaught and gave Davidson's troopers the chance to break contact and withdraw. Croxton, struggling to command his oversize brigade in the thick woods, gradually gave ground under the pressure of Wilson's advance.

Meanwhile, Forrest commandeered Brig. Gen. Matthew Ector's brigade from Walker without permission

Col. John Croxton

Maj. Gen. William Henry Talbot Walker commanded the Reserve Corps of the Army of Tennessee. He was known as "Shot Pouch" because he carried musket balls in him from wounds he'd sustained during the Seminole War and the War with Mexico.

and rushed them up to form on Davidson's right and ordered them to advance up the Reed's Bridge Road. Ector's line of advance took him around Croxton's flank and directly toward Van Derveer's brigade, formed on a ridge along the Reed's Bridge Road. "We had gone but a short distance before we discovered a heavy line of Federal infantry with several batteries just in our front," recalled Samuel Sprout of Stone's Alabama Battalion. "We had scarcely for the onset before they opened a murderous fire upon us, and we in turn upon them. The lines swayed back and forth; we would drive them and then they would drive us."

Ector advanced beyond the rest of the Confederate forces, and he sent word back to Forrest that he was concerned about his right flank. "Tell General Ector that he will not need bother about his right flank," Forrest replied.

The fighting continued with heavy losses, Ector himself being thrown to the ground when his horse went down. The Confederates moved into close range with Van Derveer and threw themselves on the ground to return fire. Private Oscar Heath of Battery I of the 4th United States Artillery recalled, "our battery was pouring canisters into the enemy's ranks and with deadly effect, for our gunners, training their guns low, and taking deliberate aim at the always visible foe tore a gap in their line with every discharge literally lifting the prostrate foes at the point of impact high in air and hurling them back mangled remains of human valor."

Ector now sent word to Forrest with concerns about his left flank. Forrest responded irritably, "Tell General Ector that by God I am here, and will take care of his left flank as well as his right."

However, Forrest did not, and soon a hail of bullets announced the arrival of a new force on Ector's flank: Brig. Gen. John King's regular brigade of Baird's division. The Confederate position suddenly seemed imperiled beyond hope.

At Jay's Mill

You are standing on the vicinity of John Jay's steam-powered sawmill, built near the little spring-fed stream to the south of the wayside panels. At the time, the field here was larger than it is today and was shaped like an inverted "L," having literally been cut out of the old-growth timber forest that made up most of the Chickamauga battlefield.

On the morning of September 19, Union soldiers from McCook's brigade made their way down from the

The engagement that began at Jay's Mill spread like a wildfire as both sides brought more men into the fight.

northwest to fill their canteens here and soon drew the attention of Confederate pickets a short distance to the south. Gunfire was exchanged as the soldiers rushed back to their commands with Confederate cavalrymen in pursuit. Soon a ragged firefight began, even as McCook was ordered to withdraw and Bedford Forrest arrived with part of his command. Events would continue to escalate as Forrest became entangled with a much larger force that caused him to bring in help from Walker's Reserve Corps.

The field at the site of Jay's Mill is smaller today than it was in 1863.

Forrest's Cavalry were not cavalry in the traditional sense. They rode on horseback, but most of his men were equipped and fought as infantry, and though they put up a stout defense, the infantry coming at them was too much for them to handle alone.

A walk out the trails to the west will bring you to a line of Georgia monuments that marks both the advanced position of Forrest's line and that of the Georgians of Col. Claudius Wilson's brigade brought to Forrest's assistance.

The monument for the 52nd Ohio of McCook's Brigade

⟶ TO STOP 3

Return to your vehicle and turn around and turn right onto Brotherton Road, making your way 0.7 miles to Winfrey Field. Pull over on the shoulder of the road on the right near the northwest side of the field, by the sign for the Baldwin Pyramid.

GPS: N 34.92480 W 85.24137

Wintrey Field

Chapter Four

SEPTEMBER 19, 1863

As the sounds of gunfire echoed through the trees, Brannan's bluecoats disappeared into the dark forest. Not long after, Brig. Gen. Absalom Baird's division moved into the woods. Baird received orders from Thomas "to push rapidly toward the left to support Colonel Croxton's brigade" which was "then hard pressed by the enemy and almost out of ammunition."

Baird's first brigade, under Col. Benjamin Scribner, pitched into some of Wilson's Georgians who seemed to melt away before them. "We . . . started them to running," recalled George Hunter of the 2nd Ohio. "We fixed bayonets and charged them. We took nearly a hundred prisoners."

At almost the same time, John King's regulars also struck the Georgians, giving Croxton the break he need to extricate his men. King then came in on Van Derveer's left and opened fire on Ector's flank, "rolling them up like a curtain," causing them to break and run. The tide of battle shifted once more as Baird cleared the woods and gave Brannan's beleaguered troops the chance to reform and make their way to the rear to resupply.

Having driven everything from his front, Scribner halted his men at a high split-rail fence bordering the large cornfield of farmer George Winfrey. The colonel of the 33rd Ohio, Oscar Moore, said to Scribner, "They can't fight us; The 'Bloody First' is too much for them!!!" All seemed to be going well—but then a hammer fell.

As first Wilson and then Ector's infantrymen went into action, the roar of battle grew steadily louder. General Walker, still with Bragg, told his commander that he was going to join his men. He also received permission to bring his other division, Liddell's, into action.

What Walker found on his arrival near Jay's Mill was not what he expected. His brigades were in serious trouble against Baird's fresh division. Now the senior

Brig. Gen. Absalom Baird

The death of Lieut. George Van Pelt, as depicted on the bronze bas relief tablet of the monument for Battery A of the 1st Michigan Light Artillery. Van Pelt was not on horseback at the time of his death.

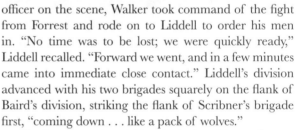

"The gallant Van Pelt was shot down at his guns, having fired 64 rounds into the midst of the enemy as they came charging down the hill . . . ."
— Col. Benjamin Scribner

officer on the scene, Walker took command of the fight from Forrest and rode on to Liddell to order his men in. "No time was to be lost; we were quickly ready," Liddell recalled. "Forward we went, and in a few minutes came into immediate close contact." Liddell's division advanced with his two brigades squarely on the flank of Baird's division, striking the flank of Scribner's brigade first, "coming down . . . like a pack of wolves."

Scribner acted quickly, deploying Lieut. George Van Pelt's 1st Michigan, Battery A and their support, the 10th Wisconsin Infantry, to face the oncoming onslaught. The 10th found themselves in a precarious situation. Deployed in front of Van Pelt's guns and lying prone on the ground on a downward slope, they opened a sporadic and ineffective fire as Van Pelt's 10-pounder Parrots fired shell and canister rounds into the onrushing gray mass to their front. Each blast from Van Pelt's guns jarred their Wisconsin support, which, with their knapsacks on, found their job becoming next to impossible as shells screeched over them. "The concussion of the guns was terrific and we were fairly bumped against the guns at every discharge," recalled August Bratnober of the 10th.

The Wisconsinites could now see Liddell's gray and brown-coated soldiers rushing upon them. "The cannon began in earnest but we could see plainly that they were firing too high," Bratnober continued. "On they came three double lines deep, then they charged . . . . Our fire fairly stunned them but we could not reload without

Col. Benjamin Scribner

rising up . . . . We had to retreat." The 10th Wisconsin broke and fled to the rear through Van Pelt's guns. Still the cannoners kept to their work as the whiz and zip of musket balls and buckshot filled the air around them. Finally, as Confederates closed in, the gunners began to rush to the rear. Van Pelt strode to the front, sword and pistol in hand, and faced the on-rushing Confederates. "Don't touch these guns!" he screamed. They were his last words. He fell beside the guns he tried to protect as the Confederates swarmed around them and howled in triumph before rushing onward toward their next target.

Federal Brig. Gen. John Converse Starkweather's brigade advanced to replace Croxton. They found the wolves rushing upon them. "All at once and without the least warning a heavy volley was fired into our ranks at a distance of about 30 yards," a private in the 21st Wisconsin said. "The Johnnies were low and therefore could not easily be seen. Oh, Shades of Jupiter! What havoc that made . . . . [T]he battery horses fell like flies, more than half; the batterey men sitting on horses and limbers were to a great part either killed or wounded. In vain did the officer who commanded the battery and the remaining men try to unlimber and bring the guns in position. We, as soon as the volley was fired, knelt down and returned the fire, loaded again and fix bajonet."

The stand was futile and brief. The Arkansasans of Govan's brigade soon overwhelmed Starkweather's, who join the steadily growing mass of fleeing bluecoats headed either north or west—anywhere they could go that was away from the Confederates.

*   *   *

Meanwhile, King's regulars, having dealt the final blow to Ector's brigade, began to tend their wounded and round up prisoners. Baird approached King and ordered him to turn his brigade to the south in the direction that Wilson's brigade was retreating. As King began the process of reorienting his brigade, Baird rode south to confer with Scribner. "We at once changed front to the rear and marched to the edge of the ravine and formed a hasty line," said one regular. "We had scarcely got into position before a division . . . advanced upon us on the run."

It was over for the regulars almost immediately. Battery H of the 5th United States Artillery only got off four rounds before the rebels were on them. The gunners fell in heaps around their guns—including their commander, Lieut. Howard Burnham. As Walthall's men moved upon them, a wounded sergeant stood and staggered to one

Brig. Gen. John King commanded the Army of the Cumberland's Regular Brigade.

Brig. Gen. Charles Converse Starkweather

Col. Claudius Wilson

"The Battery was hardly in position before, the troops on the right giving way, it was exposed to a most terrific fire of musketry from front and flank . . . . At the first fire Lieutenant Burnham fell mortally wounded."
— Lt. Joshua A. Fessenden, Battery H, 5th U.S. Artillery

of his guns, already loaded with canister, and affixed the lanyard, then drew it taunt. The Mississippians in front of the gun, seeing him, shouted to him to surrender or die. "Kill and be Damned!" he replied—and pulled the lanyard. The blast was devastating, obliterating those unfortunate enough to be in front of the gun. The sergeant paid for his bravery with his life as he was bayoneted and pinned to the ground. The other infantry regiments of King's brigade suffered a similar fate and were soon fleeing north toward the Reed's Bridge Road with Liddell's men hot on their heels.

*   *   *

Ector's Texas Brigade advanced along the Reed's Bridge Road only to have both flanks turned and suffered heavy losses.

With the repulse of Ector's brigade, Van Derveer's and Connell's brigades had no time to rest on their laurels as sound of battle heralded the approach of Liddell's men. Van Derveer quickly reoriented his men to face the new threat and Connell followed suit, then ordered the men to lie down just as King's regulars burst from the woods in a mob, streaming over and through their prone forms. "[T]he regular brigade had passed and the enemy came up, pressing them with all their might," recalled Col. Morton C. Hunter. "When within fifty yards of us the battery the 82nd Indiana opened fire and gave them a volley. Then I ordered the Eighty Second Indiana to their feet and followed up the firing as rapidly as possible,

and the battery did the same, which was so sudden and so deadly that it gave them a check; in an instant, almost, they were on the retreat."

Aiding the Confederate retreat were the men of the 9th Ohio Infantry, an all-German regiment from Cincinnati. The Germans pitched into their opponents with a wild glee, chasing them back to the abandoned guns of Burnham's battery, recapturing them. Liddell's men had pushed too far and paid the price, and now his men were in a wild retreat.

As they retreated southward, things got worse. Croxton's brigade returned to action and charged into Govan's flank, "driving them in the wildest confusion," said one soldier. Govan and Walthall's brigades now fled to the east, out of the forest into Winfrey field, and then back into the shelter of the forest beyond where they were finally rallied and reformed.

There was no rest for Van Derveer, though. Just as Liddell's threat dissipated, a new threat came from the North. Bedford Forrest dispatched a brigade in a far-too-tardy effort to cover Ector's right. The Tennessee cavalrymen swung off the Reed's Bridge Road and around the Union flank before dismounting and deploying to come down upon the flank and rear of Van Derveer and the reforming regulars. Van Derveer reacted quickly, redeploying his brigade yet again along the north side of the road. The men peered into the gloom of the forest until they saw them, "emerging from

After the repulse of Ector, Van Derveer was soon faced with a threat from the north, Dibrell's Brigade of Forrest's Cavalry. Acting quickly, Van Derveer faced his men around to confront the new enemy and drove them back.

Brig. Gen. Edward Walthall

the sheltering trees . . . and approaching us with steady tramp and desperate silence," one soldier said:

> *Our men were cautioned now to shoot to kill and we opened with file firing that soon broke up . . . the first line . . . . Our big guns were loaded with canister, which opened great gaps in the enemy's columns at every discharge, while the withering fire of the infantry was thinning their ranks at every step of their advance . . . . [T]hey began to waver at sixty yards, and at forty they broke, and they ran, every man for himself.*

With this final repulse, Walker and Forrest's men were finally played out.

However, fighting was about to begin on another part of the field as both sides now rushed more men into action.

At Wintrey Field

The chaotic nature of the battle can really be seen here as visitors will find monuments from several different parts of the battle that raged through this now-tranquil field, where deer or turkeys might be seen today.

The monument for Burnham's Battery

Make your way toward the Baldwin Cannonball Pyramid and follow the trail straight back to the monument for the 1st Michigan Light Artillery, Battery A. This monument has a bronze relief plaque showing the final moments of the battery's actions here on September 19 and the death of its commander, Lieut. George Van Pelt. However, Van Pelt was on foot at the time of his death, not on horseback as depicted on the plaque.

Although the foliage is too thick today, it still gives a fairly good idea of why artillery, the long arm of a Civil War army, was ill suited for combat here. Van Pelt's battery was made up of six 10-pound Parrot rifles, some of the best long-range guns of the Civil War—but here it didn't matter. Artillery was only as effective as the eyes of the battery commanders: if they couldn't see it, they couldn't shoot at it. So it was when Liddell's division launched its flank attack. Van Pelt had very little time to react before the "pack of wolves" was upon him.

Van Pelt wasn't the only one to share this fate. A short distance north, Battery H of the 5th United States Artillery was overwhelmed and its commander, Lieutenant Burnham, was killed as well. It would be a very bad day for artillery.

The 24th Illinois Infantry was made up mostly of German immigrants who were living in Chicago when the war began. Being one of the first regiments raised in Illinois, they were solid veterans by the time they arrived on the field of Chickamauga.

As Confederates surged through the wreck of Van Pelt's battery, they soon struck Starkweather's brigade, routed it, then moved on to route King's regulars before they were flanked in turn. The deadly game of tic-tac-toe continued as the fighting moved southward.

⟶ TO STOP 4

From Winfrey Field, continue on Brotherton Road, through the intersection with Alexander's Bridge Road, onto the Brock Field for 0.4 miles. You may park along the shoulder anywhere here. Please be sure, though, not to block traffic.

GPS: N 34.92038 W 85.24943

Maj. Phillip Sidney Coolidge of the 16th U.S. Infantry fell during the assault of Walthall's Brigade on King's Regulars. Coolidge was a scientist of note before the war. He had accompanied Commodore Perry on his expedition to Japan, then explored the new territories of the American Southwest, before finally working at the Harvard Observatory where he became the first person to observe the rings of Saturn.

$\mathcal{B}$rock $\mathcal{F}$ield

CHAPTER FIVE

SEPTEMBER 19, 1863

Listening to the steadily growing din of battle, Braxton Bragg reluctantly decided to send Maj. Gen. Frank Cheatham's massive division north to the assistance of his beleaguered troops. Reaching the Alexander's Bridge Road, Cheatham ordered his five brigades to deploy, Brig. Gen. John K. Jackson's Mississippians and Georgians—the only non-Tennesseans in the division—formed along the road. To their left, Brig. Gens. Preston Smith and Marcus Wright's brigades formed up, with Brig. Gens. George Maney and Otho Strahl's brigades being formed in reserve.

Jackson deployed his men in line of battle and then advanced westward. They went but a short distance before they came under fire from Croxton's brigade. After firing several rounds, Jackson ordered his men to charge. With a shout, they surged upon Croxton's weary men, pushing them backwards and up-slope. Croxton's men tried to push them back. "We charged the rebel lines," said one Federal, "but being overpowered after a desperate struggle for the mastery of the ground," the Union line grudgingly fell back to another ridge. Jackson pressed on, but found that this time they "failed to move them." Jackson then withdrew his men to the ridge he fought so desperately for as the rest of Cheatham's division came forward. Maney's brigade formed up to support Jackson, and Smith, Strahl, and Wright brought their brigades forward on Jackson's left.

Maj. Gen. Benjamin Franklin Cheatham

As Jackson drove back Croxton, a new Union threat moved forward: the division of Brig. Gen. Richard Johnson, ordered into action from the LaFayette Road. His lead brigades—Col. Philemon Baldwin's and Brig. Gen. August Willich's—advanced like an iron wall, "[r]ushing forward at the call of the bugle, with a cheer, the regiments drove back the rebels about a hundred yards, who then faced about and rallied around their battery,

Guns mark the final position of Capt. W. W. Carnes' ill-fated Tennesee Battery (opposite).

Brig. Gen. August Willich

**Brig. Gen. John K.
Jackson**

Brig. Gen. George Maney

determined to hold it to the last extremity." A soldier in the all-German 32nd Indiana Infantry added, "The fire became stronger and a severe battle began . . . a well-hidden battery thinned our ranks with canister. The regiment received orders to hit the dirt."

A close firefight now ensued, with Jackson's men getting the worst of it. Noticing that the Confederates' rate of fire was slacking, Willich bellowed out for his men to stand and fix bayonets, and then the blast of the bugle signaled the order to charge. Willich's men rushed forward with a yell that echoed through the ancient trees. This was too much for Jackson, who ordered his men to fall back, losing one cannon and caisson in the process.

On the Federal left, Brig. Gen. John Palmer's division also moved into battle. Palmer, at Rosecrans's insistence, deployed his brigades en echelon, a stair-step like formation, in an attempt to avoid the flank attacks that had plagued his predecessors while moving through the woods. Palmer's lead brigade, Brig. Gen. William B. Hazen's, reached the woods on the northwest side of Thomas Brock's cornfield and realigned his men just as "a storm of rifle balls," announced the arrival of more Confederates. These Confederates were under Brig. Gen. Preston Smith who had advanced cautiously through the woods along Alexander's Bridge Road on Jackson's left. Whereas Jackson ran into Willich, Smith met with no resistance.

In his firefight with Palmer's Federals, Smith's Confederates suffered heavily. "The fight was desperate," recalled Hiram Moorman of the 13th Tennessee. "The enemy were strongly positioned in thick woods." Casualties began to mount as the two sides slugged it out across the rapidly disappearing cornfield. "The battle raged in its wildest fury," one of the Tennesseans wrote. "Gen. Cheatham, the glorious old hero, could be seen galloping along the lines, encouraging the troops, and giving his orders with coolness."

The fighting only slackened as both sides began to run low on ammunition. Cheatham took this opportunity to order Smith and Jackson's brigades to retire and for two other brigades—Maney's and Strahl's—to advance to take their place. The time couldn't have been better for them because Palmer also ordered one of his brigades to make its way to the rear to resupply. Brigadier General John Turchin's men were ordered in to keep up the pressure on Strahl.

Maney stood in his stirrups and shouted, "We shall soon have an opportunity of striking again for our homes and firesides, and to acquit ourselves like men worthy of the old Volunteer State." With these words ringing in their ears, the Tennesseans rushed forward. Cheatham, hat in hand, moved along with them. Maney moved his men through the ranks of Jackson's bloodied brigade and took a position among the dead and wounded of the earlier fight—just in time to meet Willich's onrushing men. "Orders were given to lie down and fire," a solder said. Musket and artillery fire shredded Confederate ranks as the woods around the Tennesseans exploded. Limbs crashed down among them and splinters and bark pelted them. Pressure against their position mounted.

Maj. Gen. John M. Palmer

Cheatham cautioned Strahl to keep his men out of the cornfield and "make no attempt to advance." However, they did, moving into the trampled, bloody field. "I never saw so many men fall on so small a space of ground," recalled one shocked onlooker, while W. J. Worsham of the 19th Tennessee remembered, "Over this spot of ground both armies had been driven and each had left their dead and wounded to mark the ill-fated spot where the Old Nineteenth lost most of her men that day." Strahl quickly ordered his men back to the shelter of the tree line, where they returned a sporadic fire.

On the far right of left of Cheatham's line, as Jackson and Smith had their hands full, Wright's brigade advanced through the woods looking for a foe to fight. Finding nothing in Brock field, Wright began to swing his brigade to the north in an attempt to turn the flank of Palmer's division. Wright eventually came upon Palmer's flank, and the fight was on. Wright's artillery, Capt. William Carnes's Tennessee Battery, deployed on the far left to protect the brigade's flank as the infantry surged forward. They were greeted with fire from Colonel William Grose's brigade, which Palmer ordered into line on the right. Wright now had the fight he was searching for, at least for the moment, but then more Federals arrived on the scene along LaFayette Road and came in hard on Wright's flank, which had become exposed during the fight.

Brig. Gen. Richard Johnson

Johnson and Palmer, seeing that Cheatham's men were fought out, ordered their men forward for a final push. With pressure along the whole line and both flanks, Cheatham's men were pushed back steadily to the point where they had originally formed up and where Lieut. William Turner's Mississippi Battery was deployed. Turner's guns added their power to the fight, blasting rounds of double canister and shell into the oncoming blue tide, breaking the Union momentum and sending them rushing to the rear. Cheatham said that he had "never seen artillery do so fearful execution in so short a time."

Cheatham's division and his Union pursuers now settled into a stalemate as the fighting continued to spread like a wildfire to the south.

At Brock Field

The field here today is approximately half the size of the original, which would have extended a considerable distance to the south. Here, the lead elements of Richard Johnson's division clashed with Frank Cheatham's Confederates. North, in the woods, Willich's brigade shot Jackson's and then Maney's brigades to pieces.

August Willich was one of the most colorful personalities on either side during the Civil War. Born in Prussia to a Napoleonic War veteran, he attended military school and seemed on the path of many young Prussian officers until he ended up on a committee to examine "dangerous literature" written by Karl Marx and other Socialist and Communist advocates. Willich proved just how dangerous the pamphlets really were when he converted to Socialism. In 1848, when a wave of revolutions swept the Germanic states, Willich was in the forefront, leading one of the Revolutionary armies, with Fredrich Engels serving as his adjutant. The Revolution was crushed, however, and Willich found himself in exile. Traveling to London, he had a massive falling out with Marx, who he saw as having grown soft; Marx, meanwhile, said Willich was a "twice cockled Jackass." After a failed attempt to usurp Marx as the leader of the Communist movement, Willich remained a devoted Communist and immigrated to the United States in 1853, finding a hero's welcome from other "'48er refugees" when he arrived in New York City. Willich, now known as "the Reddest of the Red,"

"The firing had now become so heavy in my immediate front that I ordered my skirmish line to assemble on the left of the regiment, and fired by volley until the cartridges were nearly expended . . . ."
— Maj. J. B. Hampson, 124th Ohio Infantry

Color Sergeant Joe L. Campbell carried the colors of the 1st Tennessee Infantry on September 19th and fell near this spot where his brother later placed this monument.

A small monument marks
the position of Hazen's
Brigade on the northwest side
of Brock field.

made his way to Cincinnati and published a German-language newspaper there. Being a strong Abolitionist advocate, as were most 48ers, he was one of the first in Cincinnati to offer his services to the Union cause. When the war came, he used his fame among the former 48ers to help recruit several all-German regiments in the Midwest. Willich led one of these regiments, the 32nd Indiana Infantry, into the field. After doing well at Shiloh, he was promoted to brigadier general of the brigade that he lead into action at Chickamauga, which included his beloved 32nd. Willich never rose to higher rank, though he delivered skillful performances on other fields.

A short walk out into the
field will reveal a long line
of Tennessee regimental
monuments, placed to
show the point of farthest
advance—evidence of the
terrible cyclone of lead that
the Volunteers moved into.

Willich's tenacity helped break the northern end of Cheatham's line. The Confederate center was pinned down here in Brock field, turning the engagement into a bitter slugfest between the Union troops occupying the western wood line and the Confederates attempting to advance from the east.

⟶ TO STOP 5

Proceed on Brotherton Road 0.7 miles to the intersection with the LaFayette Road and turn right. Continue 0.22 miles to the Georgia Monument and park alongside the road.

GPS: N 34.92081 W 85.26089

A. P. Stewart's Attack

CHAPTER SIX

SEPTEMBER 19, 1863

The Confederates of Maj. Gen. Alexander P. Stewart's "Little Giant" division spent the morning of September 19 in the woods near Chickamauga Creek listening to the steady roar of battle to their left and rear. Soldiers wrote to their loved ones, played cards, or simply smoked their pipes. Around one o'clock, orders came from Bragg for Stewart "to move to the point where the firing had commended." Stewart wasn't comfortable with the vague nature of the orders, though, and rode back to confer with Bragg at his headquarters, located near the Thedford's Ford.

Bragg had been growing increasingly concerned as he came to realize that his plan was being undone by this unexpected encounter with the Federals. He explained to Stewart "that Walker was engaged on the right, was much cut up, and the enemy threatening to turn his flank, that Polk was in command on that wing, and I must be governed by circumstances." Stewart made his way back to his men and soon had them moving rapidly toward the sound of the guns. Stewart's column emerged into the southwest corner of Brock field at the height of the fighting there, just as Wright's brigade came streaming out of the woods for his first attacks.

At this point, Wright's brigade was unaware of the approach of more Federal brigades—those of Van Cleve, coming along LaFayette Road—until the Federals were nearly on top of the artillery posted on the flank to protect Wright's men. The battery of Tennesseans was under the command of Capt. William Carnes. Carnes reacted quickly and changed front to meet the unexpected threat and was soon joined by Col. John Carter's 38th Tennessee—even as the rest of their brigade began to break. Lieutenant T.L. Massenberg recalled the events that followed:

The state of Georgia commemorated its home-field advantage at Chickamauga with one of the most impressive monuments on the battlefield.

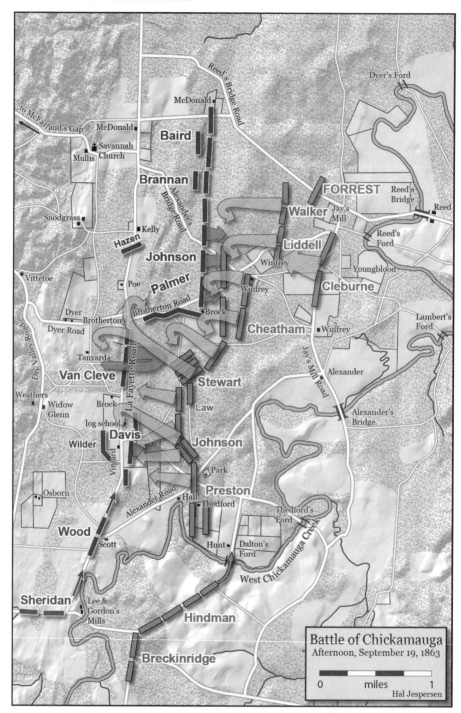

Battle of Chickamauga
Afternoon, September 19, 1863

0   miles   1

Hal Jespersen

AFTERNOON, SEPTEMBER 19, 1863—After the initial engagement at Jay's Mill, the rapidly escalating fight shifted southwest. It moved into Winfrey Field and then into Brock Field around noon.

In the heavy fighting which immediately followed, many of the men and horses were soon killed or disabled; and Carnes, seeing the impossibility of saving his guns . . . dismounted his officers and sergeants and put them and the drivers of the disabled horses at the guns to replace the cannoneers as they were shot down, and, giving the enemy double charges of canister at close range, drove back the line in his front; but as he had no support on his left, the Federals swung around the battery until it was almost surrounded. Finding it impossible to hold longer, Carnes sent his few surviving men to the rear and with his sergeant, fired his left gun a few times as rapidly as possible to keep back the fast closing lines . . . .

Maj. Gen. Alexander P. Stewart

Carnes was able to escape, but his sergeant wasn't as fortunate, riddled with bullets as he tried to mount his horse to make his escape. Union soldiers soon swarmed over the remains of the battery and continued to push toward Brock field.

Stewart arrived just in time to deal with this threat. He decided to deploy his division in a column of brigades to deal with the approaching Federals, sending his lead and least-experienced troops, Brig. Gen. Henry D. Clayton's Alabama brigade, in first. Clayton's men moved into the smoke-filled forest and soon came upon a scene of utter chaos as Wright's men streamed through

"The woods . . . was full of stragglers and skulkers and wounded," a soldier wrote.

For Brig. Gen. Horatio Van Cleve, active campaign proved too much. The 51-year-old suffered an emotional breakdown when his division collapsed on September 19. He continued in service afterwards as a garrison commander and oversaw railroad defenses.

the trees and underbrush. "The woods . . . was full of stragglers and skulkers and wounded," an officer in the 38th Alabama wrote. "Whole companies, regiments, and brigades seemed scattered to the winds . . . . The fugitives told the wildest tales of flight and massacre of regiments, and brigades 'cut all to pieces.'"

Through this throng of despair Clayton's men pushed, and then they made contact with the recently arrived Federals—Brig. Gen. Horatio Van Cleve's division. The Federals opened a destructive fire, which Clayton's men returned as best they could. "We were in a woods of dense undergrowth, and could not see the enemy 100 yards off," said one participant. "We only knew of their presence and position by the sound of their guns, and this only when they fired. A danger that can be seen frightens less than one that is invisible."

Clayton's regiments were ordered to lay down and return fire as best they could, but the contest was uneven. "Did you ever note the thickness of raindrops in a tempest? Did you ever see the destruction of hail stones to growing cornfields? Did you ever witness driftwood in a squall? Such was the havoc upon Clayton," recalled Lieut. Bromfield Ridley, a young member of Stewart's staff. Clayton's men nonetheless kept up their fire until they began to run low on ammunition, and then orders were sent for them to retire.

Now Brig. Gen. John C. Brown's Tennessee brigade was sent in. Brown's men had combat experience, but the stigma of having surrendered at Fort Donelson hung over them. Brown's men pushed their way to Clayton's former position and opened fire. "Soon the scattering shots began to fall about us, like the first heavy drops of the rain storm, gave warning that the foe was again moving to attack," recalled one of Van Cleve's men.

During the brief lull that occurred as Brown relieved Clayton, the Federals had taken the time to quickly throw down some logs to build a low breastwork behind which they were now lying. They poured fire into Brown's men, creating a "cyclone of fire," according to one member of the 32nd Tennessee. Brown's men still managed to push closer to the Federals, keeping up a heavy fire that caused Van Cleve's line to fall back to a new position, but at a high cost among their officers. One member of the 18th Tennessee noted, "our field officers were all wounded."

During the Union retreat, Cpl. James Stewart of the 75th Indiana, the color bearer of the regimental battle flag, took a wound in the right hip. "As he fell," recalled a member of the regiment, "Color-Sergeant Jacob Lair, the bearer of the Stars and Stripes of the regiment, seized the battle flag up also, and being a muscular man,

Brig. Gen. William B. Hazen was a gifted commander who couldn't stand hypocrisy and incompetence among his fellow officers. He was described by Ambrose Bierce as "the best-hated man I ever knew."

carried both flags for the moment in his hands, and Corporal Stewart on his back. In a few minutes a minie ball pierced the body of Corporal Stewart from right to left immediately under his arm pits, as he hung bleeding and wounded upon the back of Color Sergeant Lair. The shot killed the Corporal."

With the momentum finally beginning to swing, Brown was ordered to fall back to reorganize and resupply with ammunition. Stewart now saw that it was time to play his ace by sending in Brig. Gen. William Bate's hard-hitting veterans.

Bate's men had been held in reserve at the southwest corner of Brock field as first Clayton and then Brown went in. Bate now received orders to move his men into action.

The monument for the 19th Ohio

Bate rode quickly to the front of his brigade and shouted to Col. Thomas Benton Smith of the 20th Tennessee Infantry: "Now Smith! Now Smith!, I want you to sail on those fellows like you were a wildcat." The brigade rushed forward with a yell through the human wreckage that littered the woods and made their way toward the battered Federal line. "We pressed forward, unchecked by the murderous discharges," noted one of Bate's men. The howling wave of Confederates struck the Federal line "with the fury of a tornado," recalled Lieut. Marcus Woodcock of the 9th Kentucky U.S., "and we were immediately subjected to a most murderous raking fire." This was more than the Federals could take; having been subjected to focused attacks by Stewart, Van Cleve's line fell apart like shattering glass and fled for the rear, with the Confederates in pursuit.

Seeing an opportunity, Stewart now sent Clayton's men back into action, and the Alabamans rushed forward to join Bate's advancing line. As the Confederates neared the LaFayette Road, Bate's line split, with two of his regiments along with Clayton's men pushing westward into the Brotherton field, while Bate and three regiments—the 20th Tennessee, 4th Georgia Sharpshooters and 37th Georgia—wheeled to the right. Bate soon came to the edge of Poe field and saw a troubling yet tempting sight: all along the north end of the field stretched a long line of Union cannon with the gunners holding their lanyards taunt. If he could capture them, the artillery pieces would make excellent—and useful—trophies. Without hesitation, Bate ordered his men forward.

Brig. Gen. William Brimage Bate was described by one of his men as having "too little of the milk of human kindness in his composition . . . . At Chickamauga . . . he knew a major general's baton lay in his success and he would have sacrificed every member of his Brigade to attain it."

The position of Capt. Alanson Stevens's 26th Pennsylvania Battery on Brotherton Ridge

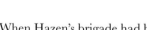

The monuments to the 79th Indiana (top) and Battery M, 4th U.S. Artillery (above)

When Hazen's brigade had been ordered back from the Brock field line, he had moved back to the LaFayette Road near the Poe farmstead. There, his men resupplied their ammunition and rested. As the sound of battle increased to the south and neared his position, Hazen formed up his men and moved southward. He soon met General Van Cleve, who was "riding wildly up the road, with tears running down his cheeks, who asked if I had any troops as they were wanted badly 'just down there,'—pointing in the direction I was going, saying he had not a man . . . . There was not a moment to spare, and my brigade, except the One Hundred and Twenty Fourth Ohio, not then reformed from the last desperate fight, was put in on the west of the road, its right thrown forward, and then generally engaged." Hazen's infantry engaged the part of Clayton and Bate that had advanced across the LaFayette Road.

Meanwhile, the rest of Bate's brigade was making its turn into Poe field against the row of Federal cannon. "There were four batteries," Hazen continued, "Standart's, Cockrell's, Cushing's, and Russell's, which I had been charged to look after, just in a skirt of timber to the west of the road between Kelley's and the field . . . . To get these in position to take the enemy's line in flank when it should uncover from the wood was scarcely the work of a minute."

Just as Bate's command emerged from the woods on the southeast side of Poe field, Hazen had formed 24 cannon along the northern edge of the field, and as Bate ordered his men to charge, the cannon opened fire.

Watching the scene develop, one of Hazen's staff, a young topographical engineer, Lt. Ambrose Bierce, recounted in the evocative style that would become a hallmark of his later literary fame:

> *The field was gray with Confederates in pursuit. Then the guns opened fire with grape and canister and for perhaps five minutes—it seemed an hour—nothing could be heard but the infernal din of their discharge and nothing seen through the smoke but a great ascension of dust from the smitten soil. When all was over, and the dust cloud had lifted, the spectacle was too dreadful to describe. The Confederates were still there—all of them, it seemed—some almost under the muzzles of the guns. But not a man of all of these brave fellows was on his feet, and so thickly were all covered with dust that they looked as if they had been reclothed in yellow. "We bury our dead," said a gunner grimly.*

Lt. Ambrose Bierce

The fire had been devastating. "Double charge after double charge of grape and canister plowed through our ranks," noted one member of the 20th Tennessee who had survived the charge. "[T]he Twentieth carried into action one hundred and forty men, and lost in killed and wounded ninety-eight, most whom fell around his battery . . . . How any human being could live through such a conflict, the good Lord only can tell." A member of the 37th Georgia, W. N. Smith, recalled, "It was here that the Federal artillery did some fine work; as soon as their men had passed to the rear they opened with canister and shrapnel, mowing down our boys at a fearful rate. The writer was with one group of ten, and at a single discharge from the battery we charging, nine went down from a charge of canister. We were so close together that I actually heard the dull thud of the iron hailstones as they struck my comrades leaving me alone and untouched."

Members of the 37th Georgia were mowed down "at a fearful rate" by Union artillery.

Bate would later report that he lost 25 percent of the men that went with him into Poe field. Bate's men sullenly withdrew into the cover of the forest from which they had advanced.

Clayton's men, meanwhile, continued to push westward, driving through the Brotherton field and gathering many prisoners as they pushed into the forest on the western border of the field. They soon emerged into the large Dyer field, and there Clayton halted. "A Staff officer reporting the enemy advancing in strong force from the right, and it also having been reported to me, through my assistant adjutant general . . . that the enemy's cavalry had been seen in force upon the left as if preparing to advance," Clayton then decided that discretion was the greater part of valor and ordered his men to fall back across the LaFayette Road. There, they were halted and reformed in connection with Bate's men, who had also withdrawn to that point.

Stewart's attack had broken the center of the Union line, but without support, he was unable to capitalize on it. However, his assault did take the momentum from Rosecrans. From now on, Chickamauga would largely be a defensive battle for Federals.

At Poe Field

A short walk will take you to the impressive Georgia monument. The monument has a color bearer on top, pointing the way to Chattanooga, while bronze sculptures ring the lower part of the monument representing the three combat branches of service: the infantry, cavalry, and artillery. From the woods here on the south end of the field, Bate's brigade had burst forth in their devil-may-care charge that shattered Van Cleve's line but then pushed too far.

Along the northern end of the field in the distance you will see a line of cannon marking the position of one of the batteries that made up Hazen's collected line, which extended across the road and into the woods on the other side. When Bate's men lunged forward in their forlorn

The Georgia monument   charge, the field in front of you would have erupted with

bouncing canister rounds and the sky above would have been filled with exploding shells—and soon the field would have been obscured by a cloud of dust and smoke. Out of this apocalypse of lead and iron, the survivors of Bate's command would stumble a short time later. Although foolhardy, no one could call Billy Bate a coward.

A line of cannon across the field from the Georgia monument marks the Federal artillery position.

In October, after a visit to the Army of Tennessee, President Jefferson Davis became one of the first visitors to the Chickamauga battlefield. As he was taken around this part of the field, he noted several dead horses. Each time, he inquired whose horse it was, and each time, he was told that each horse belonged to General Bate. Impressed by Bate's bravery and tenacity, Davis promoted him to major general and gave him command of his own division, which his old brigade became part of.

⟶ TO STOP 6

Continue a short distance north on the LaFayette Road, about 0.2 miles, and turn left onto Poe Road. Follow Poe back into the LaFayette Road and turn right. Proceed 1.1 miles to the park's designated Tour Stop 5, parking in front of the Heg Pyramid Monument.

GPS: N 34.90407 W 85.26156

Viniard Field

CHAPTER SEVEN

SEPTEMBER 19, 1863

As Stewart's division began its assault and the fighting began to wind down around the Brock field, Union Brig. Gen. Jefferson Columbus Davis's division was rapidly making its way up the dusty Dry Valley Road, approaching the home of 23-year-old widow Eliza Glenn, which was being used by Rosecrans as his headquarters.

Rosecrans met Davis and ordered him to move his brigade from the road and advance it eastward toward the LaFayette Road, south of where the roar of heavy fighting was occurring. Rosecrans wanted Davis to attempt to outflank the left of the Confederate line somewhere in the woods to his front. Davis deployed his small division of two brigades: Col. Hans C. Heg formed the left while Brig. Gen. William Carlin made the right. The two brigades advanced across the Glenn fields toward the LaFayette Road, where Heg's brigade disappeared into the forest and Carlin moved past the farmstead and onto the LaFayette Road on the edge of Tabler Viniard's cornfield. There, Davis ordered the men to lie down in the dusty road. A short distance behind them along the western edge of the Viniard farm, Wilder's brigade was deployed in a reserve, giving some comfort to Davis's men.

Heg, meanwhile, advanced through a thick swampy section of the forest. As his men struggled through vines and forest debris, moving up a slight ridge, they stumped into Confederates under Brig. Gen. John Gregg. Gregg's brigade served in the division of Maj. Gen. Bushrod Johnson, who served under Maj. Gen. John Bell Hood— the toughest-fighting commander under Lt. Gen. James Longstreet, Robert E. Lee's "Old Warhorse." Soldiers from the vaunted Army of Northern Virginia had arrived in Georgia.

Hood arrived with his division the previous evening

A soldier on the 13th Michigan monument takes aim. The regiment moved forward, "delivering a destructive fire into the enemy's massed columns."

Maj. Gen. John Bell Hood
was one of the best division
commanders in Confederate
service. A talented and
aggressive officer, he was
wounded in his left arm at
Gettysburg, only eleven weeks
prior to Chickamauga, and
was just beginning to regain
some use of it when he arrived
on the field.

and, as senior man on the field, assumed command of a temporary corps that consisted of his and Bushrod Johnson's divisions even as Longstreet oversaw the arrival and deployment of the rest of his men from the eastern theater.

Johnson's men had constructed a line of slight fortifications along a position they had established the night before. They were lounging behind those works when Heg's men suddenly appeared. Johnson's men reacted first, opening a devastating fire on the equally surprised Union soldiers. "The roar of battle became one steady, deep, jarring thunder," one Kansan noted.

The contest was quick but brutal, covering the ground with killed and wounded. Among the dead: Old Soldier, a dog that was the regimental mascot of Heg's 8th Kansas.

"Heg had inadvertently stirred up a hornet's nest," the Kansan continued, "and despite his best efforts to move them forward again, his men were soon in full retreat, stumbling back through the woods toward the LaFayette Road just as Hood ordered his divisions forward."

*   *   *

As the noise of Heg's fight roared from the woods north of Viniard field, Davis ordered Carlin to move forward into the field itself. The Federals were "advancing cautiously, but steadily" through the dry corn, one soldier recalled, when the zip of minie balls began to cut through the cornstalks as Confederates opened on them from his front and left. Carlin's advance halted and, in his words, "[t]he battle and the slaughter commenced."

Indeed it had. Moments later, Hood's advance began.

When Hood ordered the advance of his two divisions, Johnson's angled to the northwest and west in pursuit of Heg; Hood's own division, now being commanded by Brig. Gen. Evander Law, advanced to the southwest—in essence, his two divisions would crisscross in the thick woods. Why this was done remains unclear, and it ultimately weakened the blow that Hood could have delivered.

Col. Hans C. Heg, a Norwegian
immigrant and ardent
abolitionist, led a brigade
of Gen. Jefferson C. Davis's
Division.

Johnson's division, pushing forward, soon broke apart: Gregg drove back Heg while two other brigades—Colonel John Fulton's and Brig. Gen. Evander McNair's—advanced without opposition to the north. Eventually, Fulton connected with A. P. Stewart's final advance into the Brotherton field, while part of McNair's command advanced into the gap between Van Cleve's crumbling line and Davis.

Law's advance also experienced difficulties. His brigade of Alabamans disconnected from the division

The see-sawing fighting in and around Viniard field soon carpeted the ground with bodies. It was said that when the fighting ended, one could walk from one end of the field to the other without stepping on the ground.

and moved westward while Brig. Gen. Jerome Robertson, commanding Hood's famed Texas brigade, pushed his way through the forest toward Viniard field. They were followed by Brig. Gen. Henry "Rock" Benning's Georgians. As the left of the brigade emerged from the trees into the northeast corner of the field, they immediately halted and opened fire on Carlin's men, causing those Federals to grudgingly fall back toward the LaFayette Road. Robertson, seeing a great opportunity, sent word back for reinforcements.

As Heg and Carlin were falling back, Brig. Gen. Thomas Wood's division of Crittenden's corps arrived in the Viniard field from the south, having been ordered forward to assist Van Cleve. Now with a more immediate threat looming, Wood's two brigades deployed in line of battle facing to the east, with Col. Charles Harker's mostly Ohio brigade on the left and Col. George Buell's mixed bag of Midwesterners formed the right immediately around the Viniard farmstead. As Wood's men formed, their brigadier met with Davis to explain the situation—just as the 35th Illinois of Heg's brigade broke and spilled out of the woods just north of them. Wood noted that "the crisis was at hand" and, acting quickly, ordered Harker into the fight as Confederates began to move across the LaFayette Road just north of their position.

Harker moved northward up the LaFayette Road toward the flank of the still-advancing Confederates, aided by one of Wilder's regiments, the 98th Illinois. Wilder had ordered them to wheel out of their position and deal with the Confederates steadily advancing above his left flank. This was the first real action for the 125th Ohio Infantry of Harker's command, nicknamed Opdycke's Tigers in honor of their colonel, Emerson Opdycke, and their peculiar battle cry, a tiger's roar. They

Brig. Gen. Jefferson Davis bore an unfortunate name for a Union general. General Davis also bore a dark reputation. The previous year he had shot and killed his commander, Gen. William "Bull" Nelson in a Louisville, Kentucky, hotel after Nelson had berated him for a minor incident. Due to strong political ties and the Confederate invasion of Kentucky at the time, he never suffered any legal consequences for his actions—and even took Nelson's command. Needless to say, Davis was a pariah among many of his fellow officers in the Army of the Cumberland.

The woods around the Viniard farm were some of the darkest and thickest on the field, making it difficult for soldiers to see their opponents until they were mere feet apart.

advanced with a mixture of excitement and nervousness, and soon, with a tremendous volley, they announced their arrival on the Confederate flank.

Hans Heg was an aggressive commander, and even with the intense pressure on his command, he still kept trying to seize the initiative by ordering his men to advance even as Confederates pushed them back toward the LaFayette Road. Finally, it seemed to work, and a few yards shy of the road, the brigade finally halted. That, in turn, forced the Confederates of Gregg's brigade in their front to halt their pursuit. Simultaneously, Carlin stabilized his men in the middle of Viniard's field, no doubt aided in this by the presence of Buell's brigade and a line of artillery deployed to their right and rear.

Confederates countered with reinforcements from Col. Robert Trigg's brigade, who now deployed along fence line on the eastern edge of the field, awaiting orders to go in. Robertson was on the move, as well, pushing through the remains of Gregg's brigade and pitching into Heg's weary Federals. Again Heg's command fell back toward the LaFayette Road under heavy pressure. In Carlin's front, though, another Union brigade appeared, Col. Sydney Barnes' command of Van Cleve's division. The piecemeal arrival of troops on both sides continued to escalate the battle.

Barnes had stayed behind at Lee's and Gordon's Mills when Van Cleve had been ordered to move up the LaFayette Road earlier; now he was trying to rejoin his division as the action spilled into Viniard field. As he neared the fight, word from his corps commander, Crittenden, advising him that an opportunity was there

to strike the Confederate flank and ordering him "to go in and act on my own judgment." Barnes deployed his men and moved northeast into the field, coming in diagonally in front of Carlin's men.

Benning's Georgians desperately sought shelter in this gully under the galling fire from Wilder's "Lightning Brigade."

Barnes's move to strike a flank opened up his own, however—something Trigg's men quickly made clear to him. The Floridians opened a devastating fire into the right flank of the Federals. The unexpected attack was too much. Barnes's brigade broke and ran for safety right through Carlin's men. This action doomed Carlin's position, and soon Carlin's men were scrambling back toward the LaFayette Road, as well.

Trigg saw opportunity and ordered an advance into the field with the 6th Florida in the lead, but before the rest of the brigade could join them, Trigg received orders to shift to the north—so the 6th unknowingly moved forward alone. In the southeastern part of the field, a Union artillery battery—Capt. George Estep's 8th Indiana Battery—deployed, but the artillerists remained ignorant of the Floridians' approach. Fugitives from Carlin's and Barnes's brigades acted as a shield, blocking the artillerist's view of the oncoming grey line. The Confederates closed the distance and opened a devastating fire on the Indiana gunners. Estep belatedly ordered them to limber up and make a hasty retreat.

Seeing the danger, General Wood ordered one of Buell's regiments, the 100th Illinois, to charge the Floridians. Led by their one-armed colonel, Frederick Bartleson, the Illini rushed forward into the devastated cornfield. Two of Wilder's regiments joined them, ordered in by their commander to save Estep. The combined

The Heg pyramid

Brig. Gen. Jerome Bonaparte Robertson commanded the famed Texas Brigade from Lee's Army. Robertson's brigade fought with its usual hard-hitting style at Chickamauga.

counterattack proved too much for the unsupported Floridians, who now made their own hasty retreat back to the safety of the forest on the opposite side.

Now the Union line tried once more to advance. Buell ordered the rest of his brigade forward in wake of the 100th Illinois. Heg and Carlin joined in, too. Fate was against them.

Robertson's Confederates, joined now by Benning's Georgians, charged forward—and everything for the Federals fell apart. Heg's men were already past the breaking point, and with the renewed pressure—and despite their brave colonel's encouragements—they had no more fight left in them. As they fled across the LaFayette Road and across a deep ditch, Heg was shot from his horse, mortally wounded. Command passed to Col. John A. Martin of the 8th Kanasas. Carlin's and Barnes' commands also had enough and bolted for the rear, streaming through Buell's and Wilder's positions.

Robertson's men pushed forward, overrunning what remained of Captain Estep's battery and driving into Buell, forcing his men to fall back to the ditch. There, Buell attempted to make a stand, but the pressure was too great, forcing his men back even further. "We pushed ahead . . . just as the Yankee line in the field began to give way," one of Benning's Georgians noted. "We stood there shooting them down . . . . It was a horrible slaughter. The field seemed to be covered with dead and wounded."

Like Carlin's and Barnes' shattered troops before them, Buell's men fell back through Wilder's position—and there Robertson's pursuit finally stalled as Wilder opened fire, halting Confederates near the road.

Benning was now ordered forward. The Georgians pushed in among the Viniard farm buildings, into the western part of the farm, and into the fire of Wilder's Spencers. "We open fire on them, and such slaughter and carnage . . . would surely delight the demons in Hades," said a soldier in the 72nd Indiana. "A sheet of flame extends from our works to the advancing foe. The crashing of our guns is as if the foundations of the earth were being crushed. The enemy fall as grain before the advancing reaping machine."

Benning's attack quickly fell apart. The hail of bullets prompted his men to rush into the ditch for shelter, but the ditch quickly become a death trap. Gunner Henry Campbell of Lilly's Battery recalled, "Capt. Lilly moved forward two guns on the left to a position where we could take the ditch from end to end, opened out with thrible charges of canister down the ditch which compelled the rebels to retreat in confusion. The ditch was literally full of dead and wounded and proved to be a self made grave for hundreds of them."

Brig. Gen. Henry Benning was a powerful voice for secession and strong pro-slavery advocate in the years before the war.

One more command now moved into the fight: Brig. Gen. Phillip Sheridan's division. Sheridan's command was ordered up to Viniard field by its corps commander, Alex McCook. Sheridan's lead brigade, Col. Luther Bradley's Illinois brigade, approached the action from Wilder's rear, while the second brigade, Col. Bernard Liabolt's Missouri and Illinois troops, formed to their right. As the sun began to set, Sheridan's men pitched into the battle to try to claim victory in the Viniard field.

Sheridan ordered Bradley to retake Estep's guns and drive the Confederates back. They rushed through Wilder's position, cockily yelling to Wilder's men, "Make way for Sheridan!" The now-reformed brigades or Carlin and Buell joined in the attack.

The new onslaught forced the Confederates to grudgingly fall back across the LaFayette Road and into the woods beyond. Estep's guns were retaken—but that's as much as Sheridan's men could do. Confederates began pouring such a hot fire on them that Sheridan ordered them back, as they made their way through Wilder's line, they were jeered cockily, "Make way for Sheridan! Make way for Sheridan!"

Fighting finally came to a close around the Viniard farm, the fields now carpeted with the dead and wounded of both sides.

Brig. Gen. Phillip Sheridan

Riding among the devastation, Carlin experienced a particular moment of personal grief. "My poor horse waited for me to dismount; then lay quietly down in the dusty LaFayette Road and died without a struggle," he recalled. "Removing the saddle with the help of one of my men, I seated myself upon it, and then gave way to a long, hysterical crying spell, which I could not stop till I had it out."

But even the fading daylight didn't bring an end to the day's carnage. One more fight remained.

At Viniard Field

In the chaos of the fighting in Viniard Field, many men of the 58th Indiana were injured when the horses pulling the caissons of battery came crashing through their line, "crushing several men and utterly destroying all line or order in the regiment."

Here in the cornfield of Tabler Viniard, some of the worst fighting of the battle of Chickamauga occurred during a see-saw engagement in the fading light of the battle's second day. One participant noted afterwards that a person could have walked from one end of the field to the other without ever stepping on the ground. Though a bit exaggerated, the fighting here was indeed brutal.

The line of monuments along the edge of the wood-line across the road commemorates the regiments of Col. Hans Heg's brigade. Heg's men pushed into the woods here in their attempt to turn the Confederate's left flank, advancing into the Confederate line a short distance to the east.

The large charcoal-colored monument with the star on top belongs to the 15th Wisconsin. The 15th was a unique regiment for the Union army because it was composed mostly of Norwegians, with a few men from other Scandinavian countries, as well. The 15th,

The monument for the
15th Wisconsin

Traces remain of the trenches made by Bushrod Johnson's men before the fighting erupted in Viniard Field.

along with the other regiments of Heg's brigade, fought desperately here in their attempt to hold back the swarming Confederates. The 15th suffered particularly terrible losses in this fight, though, going into action with only 176 men and fielding a mere 111 the following morning—a 37.5 percent casualty rate.

Nearby is the site of a log schoolhouse that became the scene of one of the most desperate hand-to-hand fights in the battle. Members of Hood's Texas brigade smashed into Heg's line, causing some Union soldiers to take refuge in the school to resist the Confederates. The building soon became a fort, which was finally overcome by the Texans at the point of the bayonet. Scenes like this were typical in the back-and-forth fighting here and in Viniard field.

A Georgia monument stands in the background near the site of the log school house.

→ **TO STOP 7**

Make a U-turn here, being cautious of traffic, and retrace your way back up the LaFayette Road 0.9 miles to Brotherton Road. Turn right and proceed 1 mile down Brotherton Road, going through the Alexander Bridge Road intersection and then park in the parking lot immediately on the other side.

GPS: N 34.92322 W 85.24385

Cleburne's Night Attack

CHAPTER EIGHT

SEPTEMBER 19, 1863

After the Brock field slugfest, as the fighting spread southward, things remained relatively quiet on the northern part of the field. A few minor actions erupted, but mostly Thomas reformed his lines, resupplied his men with ammunition, and gave his troops the opportunity to rest.

However, a new threat moved up from the south: Maj. Gen. Patrick R. Cleburne's division of Gen. Daniel Harvey Hill's corps. Cleburne received orders to move northward from their positions south of the Chickamauga Creek to join Bishop Polk's sector and help stabilize Cheatham's position. Hill accompanied Cleburne, leaving his second division under Maj. Gen. John C. Breckinridge in front of Lee's and Gordon's Mills.

As Hill and Cleburne arrived on the northern part of the field, they were met by Polk, who decided to make one more attempt to drive Thomas back from the area around Winfrey field and turn the left flank of the Union army. Cleburne formed up his three brigades along the Jay's Mill Road, several hundred yards behind the divisions of Liddell and Cheatham. Brigadier General Lucius Polk's Tennesseans and Arkansasans formed the right; Brig. Gen. Sterling A. M. Wood's Mississippians and Alabamians the center; and Brig. Gen. James Deshler's Texans formed the left. Bishop Polk's plan was for Cleburne's fresh troops to advance through Liddell's and Cheatham's men, who would then follow behind, making the biggest Confederate assault of the day.

By the time everything was ready for the advance, the sun was setting. Cleburne's men advanced cautiously into the rapidly darkening woods.

Confederate Gen. Preston Smith and the 77th Pennsylvania Infantry met each other in the woods, and both parties came to grief.

*   *   *

Maj. Gen. Patrick R. Cleburne is regarded by many to be one of the best division commanders in Confederate service. Cleburne, a native of County Cork, Ireland, enlisted as a private and rose to the rank of major general, becoming the highest-ranking foreign-born officer in the Civil War.

As Cleburne's men formed for their attack, George Thomas had gathered the army's division commanders, minus Brig. Gen. John Brannan and Brig. Gen. James Negley, whose divisions had been sent to help stop Stewart's attack earlier. Thomas had decided earlier in the afternoon that with nightfall he would pull his men back to a ridge near the farm of Elijah Kelly along the LaFayette Road. The Kelly farm offered a better defensive position, which Thomas now showed to his commanders. He issued them orders to fall back—with the exception of Richard Johnson and Absalom Baird, who were to maintain their positions near the Winfrey field to cover the withdrawal of the others before joining them. None of them expected any more action this day.

In the trampled Winfrey field, the skirmishers of the 1st Ohio Infantry strained their eyes in the diming light as ghostly figures emerged from the woods on the eastern side. They were Wood's Mississippians. The Buckeyes raised their rifles and fired even as the Confederates moved forward—and things began to quickly unravel as their brigade lost all cohesion. Some of Wood's regiments halted to return fire while others continued forward. "Never did balls fall thicker," one of Wood's men recounted; "never did the enemy appear more stubborn. Many gallant sons went down to rise no more . . . ."

Things got worse by the minute as darkness and battle smoke made it impossible to see. Soldiers couldn't tell friend from foe. Friendly fire quickly took its toll. "In advancing and fighting in the darkness," a soldier in the 33rd Alabama remembered, "laggards persisted in shooting from the rear of the front part of the line, and some of our men killed Adjutant A.M. Moore . . . by shooting him in the neck accidentally from the rear."

Things were not going well on the opposite side of the field where Baldwin's brigade still occupied a line of hastily constructed breastworks near the spot where they had halted earlier in the day. The appearance of Cleburne's men surprised them, but they proved equal to the contest. "The fight now raged in deadly earnest," said a member of the 93rd Ohio Infantry. "The firing of musketry and artillery was one unceasing roll, while the canopy of smoke that hung like a pall overhead . . . ."

This stiff resistance—and chaos within their own ranks—caused a momentary withdrawal by Wood's men. Two batteries were brought forward to help soften the resistance, and Wood's men moved forward again, closing in on Baldwin's men. "The men loaded and fired as they steadily advanced," said one Federal, "and then in about one hundred yards of the enemy's lines they raised the rebel yell and charged the works."

The 93rd Ohio monument

The Baldwin pyramid

Philemon Baldwin recklessly rode forward to the front of his brigade and, grabbing the colors of the 93rd Ohio, moved in front of his old regiment, the 6th Indiana, intending to charge the onrushing Confederates. "Follow me!" Baldwin bellowed—and almost immediately tumbled from his horse dead. "The Regiment, very sensibly, did not obey," one of the 6th Indiana noted.

Instead, Baldwin's men broke and fled back into the forest. Wood's men followed a short distance before halting in the darkness.

To Wood's left, Lucius Polk's men groped their way through the darkness before encountering Baird's two weakened brigades. The fight that followed was short and brutal, with friendly fire on both sides. "This fire from the front, right and rear left no alternative save that or retirement in confusion and disorder," one officer wrote. Polk was unable to capitalize on this, though, as his men became just as confused and disordered by their success. They halted to reorganize their lines as Federals men made good their escape making their way back to their new position near Kelly's field.

On Cleburne's left, meanwhile, Deshler's Texans moved forward but drifted further to the left, losing contact with Wood's line and inadvertently opened a gap

Col. Philemon P. Baldwin

The 49th Ohio earned the distinction of having the highest losses of any regiment from Ohio during the war. They lost 51 men killed and wounded on September 19, along with ten missing.

in the division's line. Moving behind Deshler in support was Preston Smith's brigade of Cheatham's division, and in the darkness they did not notice the gap opening up, Smith and his staff in front. In the gloom, Smith made out the dark forms of soldiers in his front. Thinking they were skulkers from Deshler's brigade, he demanded to know who was in charge—and received a blast of musketry in reply. Smith had stumbled upon the 77th Pennsylvania, and the unhappy discovery made him the first Confederate general to be killed at Chickamauga. Smith's brigade surged forward, though, and most of the 77th were forced to surrender.

Deshler's men worked their way around Johnson's left flank and moved in for the kill, surging in upon the flank of Col. Joe Dodge's brigade as Smith's men hit their front. "Bowing our heads and grasping our guns firmly we plunged into that vortex of hell," recalled William Oliphant of the 6th Texas. "[Y]elling like demons, we dashed at the Federals and soon had them flying."

Struck on front and flank, Dodge's men panicked and fled, forcing Johnson's remaining brigade, August Willich's, to join the retreat. However, as was the case with the rest of Cleburne's division, Deshler had to halt his men and reorganize.

Cleburne drove Johnson and Baird from their positions, but the effort was unnecessary. In short time, Federals would have fallen back on their own. The sharp exchange finally brought the fighting to a close for the blood-soaked day.

At Winfrey Field

We now return to the area of Winfrey field once again just as the fighting did on the late afternoon of September 19. Night fighting was rare during the Civil War, and this fight illustrates why. Chaos reigned. Unable to see, units became intermingled, while others blundered into opposing lines; then there were the cases of friendly fire, too.

The scene of fighting earlier in the day, Winfrey field saw a second bloodbath after dark.

From the parking area, walk across the Alexander Bridge Road to the cannon marking Huggin's Tennessee Battery. A trail to the left will lead to the monument for the 77th Pennsylvania and the Preston Smith Cannonball Pyramid. These two monuments tell the story of the chaos in this forest the night of September 19. The bronze relief on the 77th's monument portrays the scene of Smith's mortal wounding.

In the dark woods, Gen. Preston Smith accidentally stumbled into the 77th Pennsylvania Infantry and, along with several staff members, was killed. The monuments to Smith (left) and the 77th (below) still tell this story.

Most of the 77th Pennsylvania was captured, with many of its officers being sent to Libby Prison in Richmond, VA, including their commander, Col. Thomas Rose. Rose later plotted and led an escape from the prison—an escape that became one of the largest and most successful escapes during the war, with more than one hundred men breaking out. Fifty-nine of them eventually made it back to Union lines. Rose was not among them, though. Recaptured, he was exchanged shortly thereafter and returned to command of his regiment.

⟶ TO STOP 8

Leave the parking area and turn right onto the Alexander Bridge Road. Proceed 1.3 miles to the intersection with the LaFayette Road. Turn right onto the LaFayette Road and then, in .08 mile, turn left into the gravel parking area for the park's Tour Stop 1.

GPS: N 34.93782 W 85.25974

Meetings in the Dark

CHAPTER NINE

SEPTEMBER 19-20, 1863

As the twilight faded into darkness and the roar of gunfire faded with it, Rosecrans and Bragg called for their principle lieutenants.

Rosecrans met his generals at his headquarters at the Widow Glenn's house. His corps commanders and most of his division commanders, between 10 and 12 men, all squeezed into the cramped log dwelling as staff officers came and went. Stress and fatigue showed on all of them, but especially on Rosecrans. The day had not gone as planned, and the result was a breakdown in corps integrity as he attempted to stabilize his lines under mounting pressure from the Confederates.

"When I entered," recalled one of McCook's staff members,

> the General [Rosecrans] was lying upon the cords of a rude bedstead at the right of the door, Gen. Thomas was standing in front of a big log fire at the other end of the room, with his coat-tails under his arms, warming himself—there was hoar frost that night; the other generals were near the fire...the situation was discussed . . . the probable amount of the reenforcements to the enemy from Lee's Army of Virginia, the plan of the next day's battle, the desperate attempts made all day by the enemy to get control of the Rossville Road. Thomas summed up the situation substantially . . . . It was further decided that the left-flank movement should be continued as on Saturday; that Thomas should hold the Rossville Road at all hazards, as the prize of the battle, and be reinforced if it took the whole army to enable him to do so . . . .

Rosecrans gave up any idea of going on the offense now, in his mind he only had one option: stay and fight. In the army's two previous encounters with Bragg—at Perryville and Stones River—the army had made a

The Florida monument

strong defense and, after repulsing Bragg's attacks, the Confederate commander withdrew. Rosecrans and his commanders now hoped for history to repeat itself.

Rosecrans ordered Thomas to continue to hold the position he had withdrawn to around Kelly field. McCook, the right wing of the army, would pull back his line slightly to the west and contract northward, shortening and strengthening the line which was 5,500 yards to 3,000 yards in length, with the southern flank of the army being anchored just below the Widow Glenn's. Crittenden's Corps would become the army's reserve, positioned in the rear and center of the army. Granger, positioned further back near Rossville, was ordered to hold his men there and be ready to come to Thomas's assistance if needed. Finally, Mitchell and his cavalrymen would cover the crossings of the Chickamauga Creek at Lee's and Gordon's Mills, Glass's Mill, and all the way back to Steven's Gap in McClemore's Cove, protecting the large field hospital at Crawfish Springs which also received orders to begin evacuating its wounded.

The meeting finally broke up. A staffer brought hot coffee in.

*   *   *

A little over a mile distant, near Thedford's Ford, Bragg was meeting with his officers too, although he didn't gather them collectively as Rosecrans did. Instead, he met with them individually.

Bragg's plan was simple: keep up the offensive. With several fresh divisions arriving, he still fixated on his original plan of turning the Union flank, cutting the Federals off from Chattanooga and pushing them back against the mountains to the southwest to crush them.

However, Bragg did make one significant change. Frustrated by the lack of coordination by his bulky high command of five infantry corps and two cavalry corps, Bragg decided to split his army into two wings. Due to seniority, Bragg gave Polk one wing, to consist of Walker's and Hill's corps, Cheatham's division of his own corps, plus Forrest's Cavalry. The other wing, consisting of Hood's and Buckner's corps along with Wheeler's Cavalry, went to Longstreet—despite the fact that Lee's Old Warhorse had not arrived on the field yet. He was, though, expected at any moment.

Meeting with Polk, Bragg informed him of his new role and told him of his plan. The attack, he explained, would be by divisions, a ripple-style assault where one division after another would rapidly move into action and have the effect of cracking the Union line from right to left, forcing them to retreat to the south west. Bragg then told Polk to initiate the engagement by attacking at "day dawn." As Polk left headquarters, Bragg retired to a nearby ambulance to rest while he awaited the arrival of Longstreet.

Longstreet had an eventful trip that day, finally arriving on his train at the Catoosa Platform, a railroad water station, around 3 p.m. He and two staff members, Colonels Moxley Sorrel and Peyton Manning, made their way toward the battlefield by following the sound and the steady stream of wounded and prisoners that made their way back toward railroad. As they neared the front just after sunset, they accidentally stumbled into Union pickets. "A sharp right about gallop, unhurt by the pickets' hasty and surprised fire, soon put us in safety, and another road was taken for Bragg," remembered Sorrel.

Longstreet met Bragg at a little after 11 p.m. even as his staff bedded down on the forest floor to get some sleep. Bragg spoke to Longstreet for about an hour, recapping what had transpired that day and informing him that he now commanded the army's left wing. Bragg then explained the plan for the next day: Polk would open the fight, withthe action to be brought on upon our right," which would then be taken up by Longstreet, who would wheel his line to the left. "With my instructions for the 20th, the commanding general gave me a map showing the prominent topographical features of the grounds," Longstreet wrote in his memoirs, "from the Chickamauga River to Mission Ridge, and beyond to the Lookout Mountain range."

With that Longstreet joined his staff on the nearby for a few hours of sleep.

* * *

Following his meeting with Bragg, Polk made his way back to his headquarters near Alexander's Bridge, where he was joined by Maj. Gen. John Breckinridge of Hill's Corps. Breckenridge's division was the freshest on the field. Only one of his brigades had slightly engaged at Glass's Mill on September 19.

Breckinridge struck a fine appearance, standing over six feet tall with steel gray eyes, coal black hair, and an impressive mustache. He was described by one admiring lady as "the most handsome man in the Confederacy."

Breckinridge was a unique figure in the Confederacy. A native Kentuckian, Breckenridge came to the army with no prior military experience yet earned a reputation as one of its best division commanders. Most of his

Maj. Gen. John Cabel Breckinridge stood over 6'2' with steel-gray eyes and coal-black hair. One female admirer called him "the most handsome man in the Confederacy."

experience had come from on a battlefield of another kind: politics. He had been President James Buchanan's vice president and was the Southern Democrat candidate in the heated presidential election of 1860.

As the two generals rode along, they soon encountered two members of Hill's staff, Maj. Archer Anderson and Lt. R. H. Morrison. Polk took Anderson aside and informed him of the new command structure and the planned attack at dawn. He also said that he wished to see Hill at his headquarters, "as the fate of the country may depend upon the attack tomorrow." The two staff officers quickly left to find their chief as Polk and Breckinridge continued on to Polk's headquarters. There, Breckinridge took leave of Polk to get some sleep while Polk wrote out orders for Hill, Walker, and Cheatham, and sent them out before heading to bed himself. The orders were quickly received by Walker and Cheatham—but not so for Hill. Hill was lost in the woods.

After Cleburne's attack had halted, Hill left his men to find Bragg. In his search through the impenetrable darkness of the forest, he arrived at Lambert's Ford, north of Alexander's Bridge, which he mistook to be Thedford's Ford. There, he waited some time before making his way back toward Winfrey field, where he ran into Maj. Anderson, fresh from his chance meeting with Polk and Breckenridge. Anderson informed Hill of the new command structure and told him that Polk wished to see him.

Exhausted and no-doubt stung by the news he would be serving under his fellow corps commander, Hill decided to take a nap, rising at about 3 a.m. to go find Polk—an adventure that proved just as successful as his earlier venture to find Bragg. Frustrated, he returned to his camp to await what was to come.

Meanwhile, while Hill made his search for Polk, Polk's courier searched in vain for Hill, unable to deliver the wing commander's orders. He returned to Polk's headquarters to report that he was unable to deliver the orders, but staffers told the courier not to disturb Polk or his chief of staff. The young private gave up and decided to get some much-needed sleep.

*   *   *

In both armies, soldiers tried to settle down after some of the most nightmarish fighting they had ever experienced. Orders were sent out to men of both sides not to build any fires—an order that made for a miserable night because of the dropping temperatures. Many of the men had been ordered to leave their

knapsacks—including their precious blankets contained within—behind as they entered the battle. Instead for warmth, many of the men huddled together and tried to sleep. The heartrending cries of the wounded drifted eerily through the forest, though, and kept all but the most exhausted men awake.

Bridge's Illinois Battery faced the full brunt of Breckenridge's morning assault.

Soldiers on both sides tried to make the best of the bad situation though. W. B. Smith of the 37th Georgia related that he and his buddies, "having each captured a fat haversack filed with ham, bacon, and other good things, concluded to have a feast, so, forming a circle, we started a small blaze, just large enough to broil some meat on a stick."

On reaching behind me to cut a stick (being in a squatting position) and throwing one foot out to the right I felt something heavy clinging to my shoe. Holding my foot up to the fire I discovered a double handful of men's brains sticking to it. Under other circumstances this could have spoiled our feast, but we had become so used to horrible sights that it would have taken worse than that to choke off an old Confederate.

*   *   *

Dawn revealed a heavy frost and thick fog across the battlefield. Arising before sunrise, Polk learned that the orders had not made it to Hill—nor could Hill be located. Polk had a new set of orders written out for Breckinridge and Cleburne to immediately attack, entrusting the orders to Capt. John Wheless, a member of his staff, for delivery. Make all haste in your mission, Polk told him.

As Wheless departed, Polk called after to him to also inform Cheatham of the delay. Wheless soon galloped out of site, swallowed by the thick fog.

Polk mounted his horse just as a member of Bragg's staff arrived to inquire why the attack had not begun. Quickly briefing the staffer about the miscarriage of orders, Polk then rode forward to join Cheatham.

Wheless arrived on the edge of Winfrey field to find Breckinridge and Cleburne with Hill having breakfast among the wreckage of Van Pelt's Battery. Dismounting, he walked forward to hand the orders to Cleburne and Breckinridge, much to the chagrin of Hill, who demanded that Wheless show him the orders. Wheless ignored this command, nonchalantly telling him that Polk "has had a staff officer hunting for you since twelve last night." Cleburne and Breckinridge read their orders and then handed them to Hill themselves. One of them suggesting that they should delay the attack since rations were them being distributed to the men. Hill agreed. Turning to Wheless, the North Carolinian said that he desired to write Polk a note and casually began to do so. In the note, he explained to Polk that he had tried to find the wing commander the night before, then offered a list of reasons why the attack shouldn't be made at that time. Wheless galloped back to find Polk and deliver the message, and soon Polk rode forward to talk with Polk himself. He heard Hill's excuses and caved in—Hill would have his way.

*   *   *

Arising early on the morning of September 20, Rosecrans rode his line. First he made adjustments to McCook's dispositions, then continued north to Thomas's sector. Thomas met him, telling Rosecrans that he needed more men to extend his line further to the north to cover the intersection of the LaFayette and McFarland Gap Roads, an important route back to Chattanooga. The Virginian requested Gen. James Negley's division, part of his corps then occupying part of McCook's front line. Rosecrans agreed and sent word to Negley to move and for McCook to replace them.

Time passed and, with the sun rising, Thomas sent orders to Negley to move immediately. Negley received them just as McCook sent similar orders to move "if practicable." Negley determined that he should immediately go, even though no replacement troops

were present, ordering his reserve brigade, Col. John Beatty's, to lead the way.

Once Beatty was on the road, Negley began pulling his two front-line brigades out, but then Rosecrans arrived. The army commander ordered Beatty to continue onward but otherwise ordered Negley to stop. Return the front-line brigades into position, Rosecrans said, snapping at the division commander to await replacements before opening a gap in the line. Rosecrans sent word to Crittenden to send forward one of his divisions to take Negley's place and then rode off to confer with McCook.

John Beatty arrived with his tired troops on the northern end of Thomas's position and was moving his men into line when word arrived from Thomas to continue on northward another quarter of a mile toward the farm of John McDonald, on the north side of the McFarland Gap Road intersection. Beatty, not one to hold his tongue, called the move "decidedly unwise." Beatty was reassured that he would soon be joined by the other brigades of his division.

Leaving part of his artillery to cover the south end of his line, Beatty grimly moved into the open field of the McDonald farm, detaching his regiments along the way to try to cover the vast distance he'd been assigned. Yards separated each of his units. Beatty realized that there was no way he could hold this line if attacked before the rest of the division arrived, so he ordered a heavy skirmish line advanced into the woods east of the field.

The skirmishers were just moving into position when

The 5th Company, Washington Artillery from New Orleans was one of the best artillery batteries in the Army of Tennessee. Many of its members were young men from high society. Led by Capt. Cuthbert Slocomb, the gunners of the 5th Company fired a staggering 682 rounds in three hours from its six cannon in support of the Confederate assaults on this part of the field.

Capt. William Cockrum of the 42nd Indiana, an ardent abolitionist and prewar Underground Railroad member, was severely wounded in the early moments of Breckinridge's assault. Cockrum was shot through his hips and left on the field with the rout of Beatty's Brigade and captured, ending up in Libby Prison in Richmond, Virginia.

they were greeted by the ominous sound of thousands of men making their way through the forest.

Harvey Hill had finally ordered his men forward.

Around 9:40 a.m., nearly four hours after the attack was supposed to start, Breckinridge's division—consisting of Brig. Gen. Daniel Adams's Louisiana brigade, Brig. Gen. Marcellus Stovall's mixed brigade of North Carolinians, Georgians, and Floridians, and the famed Orphan Brigade of Kentucky led by Brig. Gen. Benjamin Hardin Helm—moved forward.

The rattle of musketry soon announced that the fight had finally began. Beatty faced two and half brigades with his one, and the odds soon began to show as his skirmish line burst from the woods in headlong retreat with a tidal wave of Confederates in pursuit. A member of one of Stovall's Florida regiments recalled that they "swept through the woods . . . driving the Yankees like sheep." After a short but desperate struggle, Beatty's line collapsed and fled westward, though some men did rally around the guns of a single battery that was pouring canister and shell into the onrushing Confederates. The artillerists managed to escape with all but two of the battery's guns, which were overrun by part of Helm's Kentuckians.

A short lull ensued. Adams's and Stovall's

Confederate brigades swung their lines to move south against the flank of Thomas's line.

The Confederates' main push was coming.

At McDonald Field

In the middle of McDonald farm, visitors can see to the east the lone monument for the 104th Illinois behind the Florida State Monument, a part of Beatty's ill-fated line. They alone would face Stovall's brigade as the Confederates burst out of the eastern edge of the forest. You can walk across the LaFayette Road here to get a better perspective, but be careful of the traffic along the road in this area.

Along the south end of the field you can see four cannon marking the final position of Bridge's Illinois Battery. A trail leads to these guns that faced the full weight of Breckinridge's division.

There had to be some irony to John Breckinridge's decision to become a Confederate general. The former vice president hailed from a prominent Kentucky family with a Revolutionary heritage. Now the man who had once sought to become commander in chief of the United States military was leading troops against it. Despite having no prior military training he proved to be one of the better division commanders in the Army of Tennessee, and the skill with which he handled his division on the morning of September 19 proved that as they smashed into John Beatty's men and then wheeled to the south to assault Thomas's flank. Breckinridge was a hands-on officer and followed close behind his lines.

On the southern end of his line was his pet brigade, the 1st Kentucky Brigade—or as it was more famously known, "The Orphan Brigade."

The 15th Kentucky monument

As he advanced, the Orphans' line split, with part of the brigade striking Thomas's fortified line just to the south and east while the rest of the brigade continued to advance with the rest of the division, striking a regiment of fellow Kentuckians, the 15th U.S. Regulars. The Kentuckians burst out of the woods on the south end of McDonald field to strike the Union line that had formed around Bridge's Battery; the Kentuckians swarmed over the guns before they could make their escape.

The Kentuckians used their trophies to earn a little redemption. Earlier in the campaign, "[t]he Kentuckians were poorly supplied with axes, and no suitable wood was in reach; so, considering the last order so imperative as to supersede the first, they promptly pounced on the fence and made the necessary fires. The citizen

reported at headquarters, and General Breckinridge rode down to the bivouac in a white heat and scolded the men, in rather unmeasured terms, calling them "a lot of vagabonds and thieves." This was too much for the Kentuckians. They thought the exigencies of the case justified the destruction of the fence, and they were angry— and they nursed that anger. Now, "[w]hen the brigade had made its last charge and taken the fine battery near the road which they struck when they went over the Federal position, some of them ran one of the guns forward, and just as Gen. Breckinridge and staff reached that point, elated over the victory and congratulating the men, Eph Smith, of the Fourth Kentucky, sprang astride one of the cannons, swung his cap over his head, and cried out: 'Gen. Breckinridge, see what your thieves and vagabonds have stolen!' This brought the General to a standstill and a shade to his brow, and he rejoined: 'My brave boys, you misunderstood me! I didn't say it. I said that people would consider you thieves and vagabonds!' That was enough. Breckinridge resumed his place in their affections."

Monument to the 42nd Indiana on the ground where they were overwhelmed by the brigades of Adams and Stovall.

Recalled one victorious Kentuckian, the rest of the Orphan Brigade was having a much harder time a short distance away as the rest of Breckinridge's division surged around Thomas's flank.

⟶ **TO STOP 9**

Turn right onto the LaFayette Road and then turn left onto Alexander Bridge Road. Proceed .03 miles to the intersection with Battleline Road and turn into the parking lot there.

GPS: N 34.93331 W 85.25536

Thomas's Battleline

CHAPTER TEN
SEPTEMBER 20, 1863

The morning of September 20 ended a miserable night for the soldiers of Thomas' Corps, frozen as they were by the frost, with the fog as the only blanket covering any of them. Although dawn meant another day of fighting, they were pleased to see the sunrise.

As the men began to stir and prepare their meager rations of salt pork and coffee, Col. Isaac Suman of the 9th Indiana Infantry went to his brigade commander, General Hazen, and suggested that they construct a breastwork along their line. "I at once gave orders that one rank work at this while the other stood to arms, and went to urge the commanders to my left to do likewise," Hazen later recalled. Soon, the entire line was at work, dragging out logs, rocks, fence rails, and knapsacks. Although not especially impressive, being only two to three feet high in most places, it was still enough for a soldier to lie down or kneel behind. One soldier in the 2nd Ohio noted that these makeshift works "saved many a life that day."

Thomas also strengthened his line by deploying his troops in accordance with the new tactics manual that the army had adopted earlier in the year, *Casey's Tactics*. The manual called for each brigade to deploy with two regiments in front and two regiments directly behind them in reserve where they could react to a threat from either flank or the rear.

As Thomas's men prepared for battle, Breckinridge began his attack on their left. The sound of battle told Thomas's men that they would soon be engaged. Baird's division, positioned at a critical bend in Thomas's line, were first to see the advancing Confederates. The blue flags of the left wing of Helm's brigade headed straight at them through a large open cedar glade.

Brigadier General Benjamin Hardin Helm presented a very cavalier appearance, riding along his lines on a

The monument to the 2nd Ohio Infantry took its design in honor of the XIV Corps, which adopted an acorn as their symbol following the campaign for Chattanooga. The acorn was chosen by Gen. Thomas because his men stood like oaks at Chickamauga.

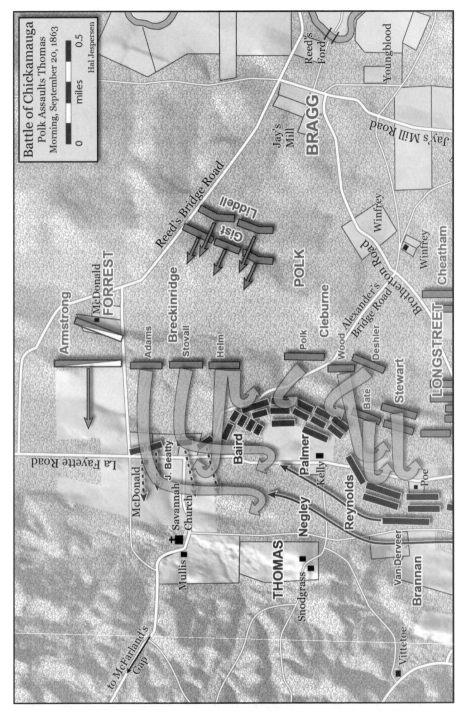

POLK ASSAULTS THOMAS—When the Confederate Attacks finally began on the morning of September 20, they struck furiously against Thomas's defenses but were unable to break the fortified line. The early morning delay proved to be fatal for Bragg's plan of turning the Union left flank and cutting them off from Chattanooga.

white horse, encouraging his men onward. At 32 years old, he was a West Point and University of Louisville graduate. The son of a former governor of Kentucky, an officer in the Kentucky State Guard, a member of the state's House of Representatives, and the state attorney for his district—Helm was a rising star. It was fitting that he courted and married a young lady from a prominent family: Emilie Todd, the baby half-sister of Mary Todd Lincoln. In 1861, Hardin Helm found himself in a very unenviable situation: his Todd brothers-in-law and friends urged him to side with the Confederacy, and his father and brother-in-law, President Abraham Lincoln, urged him to side with the Union. Lincoln even sweetened the deal by offering Helm the post of paymaster, but ultimately Helm sided with the Confederacy.

Brig. Gen. Benjamin Hardin Helm commanded the ill-fated Orphan Brigade at Chickamauga.

As Helm's Kentuckians charged forward, they came under a destructive fire from their front and left. "We were laying behind our rude breastworks, two regiments deep, and the rebel columns soon appeared over the hill," said Sergeant Samuel Price of the 2nd Ohio. "On they came amid the shower of musket balls, grape, and canister pouring from our lines." The destructive fire was too much and stopped the Confederates 75 yards short of the Union line. They retreated in "wild confusion," but Helm was there to rally them and get them to try again. Raising the Rebel Yell, they surged back over the crest of a low rise and back into the hellish fire of Baird's line, giving "their lives in reckless fashion."

The fire of the 4th Indiana Battery did enormous damage to the Confederate attackers. Both Gen. Helm and Col. Colquitt were mortally wounded by the fire of these guns.

Along the Union lines, the men kept up their deadly work. Deployed in a line two regiments deep, the front regiment laid down and fired over their logs while a few yards behind another regiment laid low and, when loaded, stood to fire over the men in front of them. The fire they unleashed into the "Blood of Boone" was catastrophic. Men tumbled to the ground in heaps along the small rise. Helm's second attack faltered, but once more he rode among his men, encouraging them to go forward—but this time, as he rode forward with them, an artillery shell exploded nearby and a piece of struck him in the side, causing him to slide from his horse mortally wounded. Helm's men carried him from the field, and he perished that night, leaving his brigade orphaned once more. Colonel Joe Lewis of the 6th Kentucky assumed command and ordered the brigade back to reunite and reform.

While Helm slammed his brigade against the defenses near the angle of Thomas's line, Adams and Stovall moved into action against Thomas's flank. Deployed on both sides of the LaFayette Road, they rolled southward through McDonald field. Adams's brigade entered the woods on the west side of Kelly field

Few trees remain of the once-large cedar grove that Helm's Kentuckians advanced through.

35th Indiana Infantry was distinctive for being an Irish Regiment. The Irishmen fought desperately to defend their part of Thomas' battle line on the morning of September 20th.

and made their way forward through the woods driving fragments of Beatty's brigade before them; Stovall moved his line through a skirt of woods, forcing the flank of Thomas's line to refuse back. Stovall then pushed on and struck Col. William Grose's brigade, which was being ordered up to extend the Federal flank. Grose's men were deploying when "we heard a heavy body of troops come marching through the underbrush and leaves," wrote one member of the 6th Ohio,

> *but nothing could be seen, until suddenly a gray line burst into view, and, before we were aware of it, fired into us a terrific volley. Fortunately we were lying down at the time . . . Then the game began in real the two lines scarcely fifty yards apart, and each firing as fast as possible...*

Grose's brigade, facing fire from both Stovall and Adams, broke and retreated into Kelly field. Breckinridge had turned the flank and was moving into Thomas's rear just as Bragg had planned.

The doorway to victory was opening.

*   *   *

As Stovall's men emerged from the forest, they were stunned to suddenly see a Union brigade appear as if out of the ground a few yards in front of them. Van Derveer's brigade had arrived a few moments before and had been ordered to lie down. Now, as Stovall's graycoats entered the field only 75 yards away, Van Derveer bellowed for them to rise and fire "a murderous fire almost in their faces." The blast staggered Stovall's line and ground their advance to a halt. They were ordered to lie down along the field's edge and return fire—even as Union artillery came into action further to the south. "For a short time the 47th was halted in the open field under the terrible fusillade of shot and shell from the batteries and rapid fire from the lines of supporting infantry," recalled Adjutant Benjamin Williams of the 47th Georgia. "Our flagstaff was cut in two and our colors riddled . . . . "

Pressure mounted as Union artillery batteries in the middle of the field turned and opened fire, causing the air above the Confederates to become alive with flying iron. All along Thomas's line, regiments from his second line were turned to face the new threat. The maelstrom proved too much, and Stovall's brigade fled to the rear.

As Stovall's line met Van Derveer's, Adams's Louisianans pushed on until they met their own ugly surprise: Col. Timothy Stanley of Negley's division. Advancing through the woods, the cheering Confederates suddenly saw Union regimental flags rise in front of them from behind a screen of brush and brambles. At a distance of about 50 feet, "a sheet of flame went from the muzzles of our guns, and a windrow of dead and wounded Confederates lay on the ground." Among them: the portly form of General Adams, knocked from his horse with a serious wound to his left arm.

Command of the Louisianans passed now to Col. Randall Gibson, who ordered them to retreat. Stanley shouted for his men to charge, and the retreat became a rout. Stanley's men pursued until they entered

The 60th North Carolina Infantry of Stovall's Brigade pushed into the northern end of Kelly field, along with the rest of their brigade, only to be stopped by the arrival of Union reinforcements.

A bas-relief image of the fighting across Kelly's field

"For some twenty-five minutes," said Gen. Gist of the 24th South Carolina, "the gallant little band withstood the terrific fire and returned it with marked effect . . . ." The 24th lost 169 of its 410 men during those 25 minutes. Among the wounded were the regiment's colonel, lieutenant colonel, major, and many of its company officers.

McDonald field when they came under fire of Adam's artillery support, the 5th Company of the Washington Artillery. Firing rapidly, the six cannon drove Stanley's men back into the cover of the woods.

Breckinridge's division was done. They had achieved Bragg's goal, but with the arrival of Union reinforcements and without support, Breckinridge could go no further.

*   *   *

As Breckinridge moved down the LaFayette Road in the wake of Beatty's shattered brigade, Polk ordered in Walker's divisions, but the arrival of Hill stopped this. Hill had noticed that as Breckinridge advanced, a wide gap opened in the middle of his corps, and he needed one of Walker's brigades, specifically that of Brig. Gen. States Rights Gist, to fill the hole.

Gist was the son of a rabid South Carolina Fire Eater—ergo the son's actual name, States Rights, which was not just a nickname. Following in his father's footsteps, Gist served as an advisor to the South Carolina governor during the Secession Crisis. He was also present for the firing on Fort Sumter, and he served as an aide to Brig. Gen. Bernard Bee at Bull Run. He then returned to South Carolina to accept command of his own brigade.

Gist's brigade had missed the first days of the battle of Chickamauga, and due to a battlefield promotion for Gist to command Walker's old division, command went to his senior colonel, Col. Peyton Colquitt. Colquitt was the son of a Georgia Supreme Court justice and Fire Eater. He had attended West Point but flunked out, so he became a newspaperman and outspoken supporter of secession in his hometown of Columbus, Georgia. He had led some of the first troops from Georgia to Virginia in 1861 before returning to take command of his own regiment in 1862.

Hill now summoned the regiment, and Polk complied. Told he was going to support Breckinridge, Colquitt led his men along the same path as Helm and straight into an ambush. His men blundered into the angle of Thomas's line and came under "a concentrated . . . murderous fire" that forced the brigade to hit the ground and try to find what cover they could. Colquitt ordered them to "keep up an irregular fire." It would be one of the last orders he'd give. He was struck in the chest, just like Helm before him, and mortally wounded.

The loss of officers soon became keenly felt all along the line. One regiment, the 24th South Carolina, lost its colonel, lieutenant colonel, major, adjutant, and most of its company officers in a few minutes' time. Walker had to send forward his two remaining brigades, Ector's and Wilson's, as a distraction, to help everyone make their escape. Gist's brigade lost over 300 men in less than 30 minutes of combat.

Walker still had Liddell's division to send to Breckinridge's aide, but Polk grabbed Walthall's brigade and ordered them to the assistance of his nephew, Lucius Polk, leading a brigade in Cleburne's division. This left only Govan's Arkansas brigade, which rushed forward through Breckinridge's retreating men. Govan pushed on into the woods on the northwest side of Kelly field, but the numbers he faced were overwhelming and the brigade was forced to retreat.

The day remained early, but already, Thomas was showing a steadfastness that would soon prove essential.

At Thomas's Line

The line of monuments here follows the line of Thomas's breastworks on the morning of September 20. Though never very impressive, they were enough for Thomas's men to lie down or kneel behind for protection from the storm of incoming bullets. Many of

The line of monuments today follows Thomas's line of crude breastworks.

Many of the monuments in this area illustrate men kneeling or layng behind log barricades. By the time of the battle of Chickamauga, both armies were changing the ways they fought in battle, no longer simply standing up shoulder to shoulder, trading fire.

the monuments illustrate these fortifications: you will see them carved in stone on the monuments to the Regular Brigade and on the bronze relief plaque on the 33rd Ohio's monument.

We tend to think that Civil War soldiers always fought standing in long lines, elbow to elbow, advancing like toy tin soldiers, but that wasn't always the case. Indeed, at Chickamauga there are few accounts of men standing and fighting other than for advances. "The citizens of today will doubtless wonder how any man could escape such a rain of shot and shell, but by the old soldier it is readily understood," noted one Orphan, Lt. Lot Young of the 4th Kentucky. "While ninety per cent of these shots were being fired the men were lying flat on their faces and were overshooting each other when suddenly one or the other would spring to his feet and with a bound and a yell rush at a double-quick upon their foe . . . ."

Colonel Benjamin Scribner, a Federal on the defense here, recalled:

A monument marks the furthest point of advance of one of the Orphan Brigade's regiments.

> *We formed in two deployed lines along a wooded ridge, behind us an open field, and before us the ground sloped away from view in the timber. Our division was on the extreme left of the army and covered the road to Rossville and Chattanooga. The Third Brigade was on my right and the regular brigade on my left. We hastily threw up breastworks of rails and such logs as could be found, in front of each line. The second line, owing to the declivity of the ridge, was very near the first. These dispositions had scarcely been made, when the enemy commenced a furious assault upon us. I instructed my second line to move to the works of the first and deliver their fire after the first, by my order, should commence to fire, then each was to load his musket shielded by the same shelter, and thus*

to alternately load and fire while the conflict lasted. The enemy prepared for this attack with much deliberation. Their battle flags (a white ball on a dark field) were planted along their line to form by, and their officers, with swords held across their breasts with both hands, facing their men, dressed their line with commendable coolness and vim. When they got ready, they made a dash upon us. We had reserved our fire while they were making these preparations, but now we gave them a warm reception with an incessant outpour of bullets. The battery of the Third Brigade had a flank range along my front by some of their guns. This range was a narrow open space covered with green, mossy grass. In this space we held the enemy while the battery mowed them down.

The nature of battle was changing. The soldiers were learning and perfecting a field craft that will lead to the trench warfare of the final campaigns of the war.

⟶ TO STOP 10

Continue down Battleline Road 0.4 miles until you see the signs for the Deshler and King Cannonball Pyramids. Park in the pullover across from the Texas Monument.

GPS: N 34.92716 W 85.25644

A stack of cannonballs marks the spot where Col. Peyton Colquitt, commanding Gist's Brigade, was mortally wounded as his command went into action (below, left). Other officers, such as Gen. Helm (below, right), also have cannonball pyramids marking the locations of their mortal woundings.

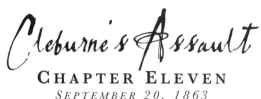

Cleburne's Assault

CHAPTER ELEVEN

SEPTEMBER 20, 1863

As Breckinridge's men rolled into battle, so did Patrick Cleburne's.

Advancing in a single line, Cleburne's division moved forward just to the left of Helm's brigade, running into trouble almost from the beginning. Cleburne's two left brigades became entangled with Stewart's division of Longstreet's wing, which had been moved northward earlier in the morning. This caused Polk's brigade to strike the Union line alone and unsupported—with predictable results. Advancing unseen until cresting a slight ridge about 100 yards from the Union line, Polk's brigade was greeted by what one Tennessean remembered as "a terrible burst of artillery and musketry . . . . The hissing of the missiles was more noticeable than the explosions of the guns, and sounded like the clashings of a multitude of sword blades in the air overhead . . . ." Lycurgus Sallee, a member of the 1st Arkansas added, "As we emerged from this ridge . . . the whole command and artillery fired, creating a smoke that nothing could be seen in."

The line soon halted, and the Tennesseans were ordered to lie down and return fire. As Polk tried his luck, Wood's brigade moved against the line farther south, with part of his brigade striking parts of Joe Reynolds's and John Brannan's divisions. The attack caused Wood's line to split, with half going around the end of the line toward the Brannan's line along the western edge of the LaFayette Road. "The command [to] charge was given almost at the same moment the enemy opened a fire of small arms, shot, shell, and canister so well directed that it compelled our regiment to seek protection in the bushes," one Alabamian noted; "they were ordered to lie down, but having no protection were killed by the dozen."

Not being able to strike either line with full force doomed the attack to failure, and with heavy loss they

The Texas monument

Brig. Gen. Lucius Eugene
Polk commanded a brigade
of Tennesseans and
Arkansasans in Cleburne's
Division. Polk was the nephew
of General Leonidas Polk.

retreated. Lieutenant William McCaskey of the 79th Pennsylvania wrote, "The rebel hordes charged, and recharged upon our brigade . . . but we sent them back, and covered the earth with their dead."

Deshler's Texans found their way into the gap that had opened between Wood and Polk and advanced to try their luck. "The rain of lead that the Federals poured into our line was simply terrific," one Texan officer remembered. "Our loss in officers and men for the first few minutes was alarming in the extreme . . . . [W]e were ordered to lie flat down and hold it. In a very short time the men were out of ammunition."

The men pressed themselves to the ground as a storm of artillery sprayed the area with iron. One Texan described their ordeal:

> *Shells burst over us, under us, and in our midst. Balls of all sizes, grape, canister, and 6 and 12 lb. balls, whizzed among us in copious profusion and fearful proximity. One man in our Company was struck down by a grape, and another had his shoulder torn off. A 12 lb ball went through Co. B (next to us) took off one man's head, and tore two others to pieces!*

During this crisis, as the brigade commander, Brig. Gen. James Deshler, moved down the line to check the ammunition of the men, an artillery shell struck him in the chest, hurling his body back through the air. "His heart was literally torn from his bosom," cringed Col. Roger Q. Mills of the 10th Texas, who then assumed command of the Texans. Mills wisely kept his men hugging the ground.

Fighting in the woods

Cleburne had little more luck against the Union barricades than Breckinridge had. Both of Walker's divisions were broken up, too. Bragg saw everything falling apart again—his simple plan was not being followed and now, instead of victory, it seemed that defeat was seizing the day.

Bragg knew something had to be done and quickly, so he ordered his staff to bring the left wing into action. Taking no chances, though, he sent the orders not only to Longstreet, as wing commander, but to each division commander separately: bring everyone into action down the line.

At Cleburne's Assault

Shortly after Breckinridge's assault began, Cleburne advanced his division against the center of and lower part of Thomas's line—and met the same fate that Breckinridge had earlier. You will note the Texas monument here, though no Texans were able to get this close to the Union line.

A short walk down the trail behind you will lead to the cannonball pyramid for Brig. Gen. James Deshler. Deshler's Texans tried several times to assault the Union line, but the combined fire of rifles and artillery halted them along the slight ridge here. Finally seeing that the attack was going nowhere, the brigade was ordered to lie down and return fire as best they could. The following contest was unequal, but the Texans endured as best they could, hugging the ground and firing at any movement

Fighting in the deep forest proved disastrous for artillery units, which were only able to engage at close range. It made them easy targets for infantrymen.

Brig. Gen. James Deshler was the son of a strong radical secessionist who told a northern-born friend that ending slavery would destroy the South economically, and "putting us down upon a platform of perfect equality with our own chattels. How can we stand the proposition? . . . You would die first. Well, so will we . . . ." His son did.

they could see above the line of logs and rocks that marked the Union line. After some time, the fire of the Texans slackened, and Deshler began to check their ammunition supply, walking down the line of prone men and randomly checking their cartridge boxes. A Federal cannon boomed, and a shell hurled forward, striking Deshler and killing him.

Deshler's death was like a Shakespearian tragedy for his father, David Deshler, who had already lost one son, his wife, and his daughter in the years leading up to the war. David planted the seeds for the bitter fruit that was borne to him with James, though. Despite being a native Pennsylvanian, David had become thoroughly radicalized by living in north Alabama, where he had amassed a small fortune in the railroad business. In February 1861, as war clouds loomed, he wrote to a friend in Philadelphia: "You don't seem to see that the Black Republican programme would be degradation, socially and politically to our section; it would be the destruction of $4,000,000,000-four thousand millions of dollars-of property to us, besides putting us down upon a platform of perfect equality with our own chattels. How can we stand the proposition? Could you agree to it, supposing that we changed places? Not at all-You would die first. Well, so will we . . . ." David thoroughly imparted this same view to his son, who resigned from the United States Army and joined the Confederate service, rising to the rank of brigadier. Following James's death, David Deshler was left alone in the world with his fortune. By the end of his life, he had not softened his views, though. His will even displayed his unending hatred for his Yankee roots, setting forth that none of his nephews who had served in the Union armies would receive any inheritance from his estate.

Col. Isaac Suman of the 9th Indiana Infantry, whose men were the first to start barricading their line early on September 20. Soon, other regiments began to do the same, and before the Confederates attacked, Thomas's entire line was behind log and rock barricades.

⟶ TO STOP 11

Continue on Battleline Road for 0.4 miles. Cross over the LaFayette Road and onto Poe Road. Proceed down Poe Road 0.16 miles until you reach the wayside exhibit. Park in the spaces provided there.

GPS: N 34.92216 W 85.26220

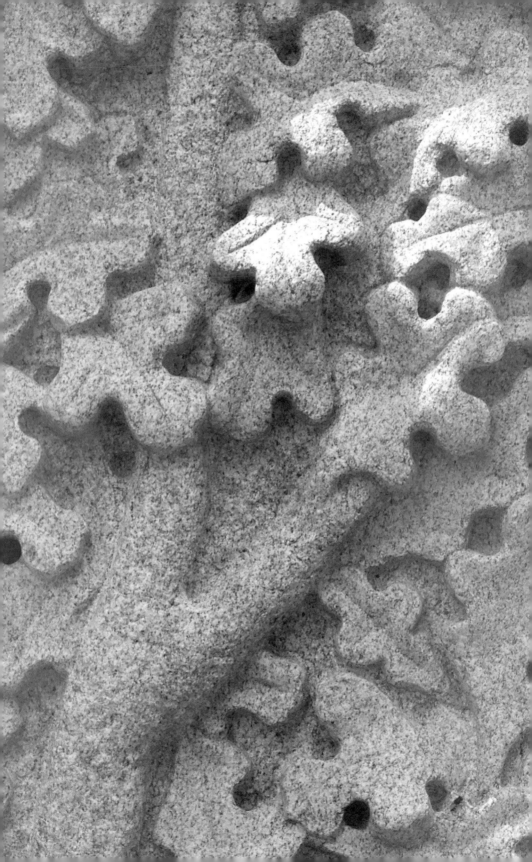

Poe Field Redux

CHAPTER TWELVE

SEPTEMBER 20, 1863

Polk's assault that morning had been a huge failure plagued by chaos and ambivalence, but it sent shockwaves through the Union command and unwittingly set the stage for disaster for the Union army.

Under repeated assault, Thomas had started sending a stream of staff officers for reinforcements, prompting Rosecrans to start forwarding units from the rest of the army. One unit that Thomas called upon was the division of John Brannan—the troops who had started the fighting the day before near Jay's Mill. Brannan had been designated as a reserve for Thomas the night before, but early on the morning of September 20, Rosecrans ordered him to move forward from his position in the north end of Dyer field to the front line to fill in a gap between Negley and Joe Reynolds. Thomas was not informed of this move, though, and now because of Polk's attacks, he sent for Brannan.

The task of delivering the message was in the hands of Capt. Sanford Kellogg, who found Brannan around 10 a.m. as the fight against Wood's Confederates was going on.

Brannan read the orders and was immediately concerned. He feared that his move would expose the flanks of the divisions to either side. With Kellogg accompanying him, Brannan rode to confer with Joe Reynolds, who commanded the next division up the line. Reynolds was not thrilled by the change, but he approved the movement. Turning to Kellogg, Reynolds said the young captain must report to Rosecrans that the move could potentially lead to danger. Kellogg immediately galloped off to find Rosecrans, and Brannan rode back to his command to start the process of moving them out.

In the woods east of Poe field were A. P. Stewart's three battered brigades. Just as Brannan was returning to his division, Stewart received orders to go in. The woods on the eastern edge of Poe field exploded with a wave

Capt. Sanford Kellogg, a member of Thomas's staff and also his nephew by marriage

Battery D, 1st Michigan Light Artillery, commanded by Capt. Josiah Church, "engaged the enemy as they advanced. I had an enfilading fire on a portion of their advance, and by hard firing for about fifteen minutes I succeeded in checking the enemy . . . ."

Larkin Poe was a very poor tenant farmer, living on property owned by his father-in-law, George Brotherton. Poe was conscripted into the Confederate Army, serving in a cavalry regiment. Although he wasn't present for the battle, he arrived a short while after to find his cabin had burned to the ground during the savage fighting that swirled around it.

of gray and brown-clad soldiers headed with reckless abandon straight for Brannan's line. Brannan now lost all thought of following Thomas's order and set about repulsing Stewart's onslaught.

Earlier that morning, Rosecrans had left Eliza Glenn's home, advising the young widow to leave, and moved his headquarters further north to a knoll just behind the center of his line, only 600 yards from the front line. This is where young Kellogg found the army commander and delivered word that a gap was being made by Brannan's withdrawal and that Reynolds desired protection for his flank. Rosecrans's headquarters was a hive of activity as he juggled units about and funneled more units to Thomas's assistance—indeed, it seemed as if he was reinforcing Thomas with the rest of the army. Orders were at that very moment being written out by his chief of staff, Gen. James Garfield, for Sheridan to move his division from the extreme right to reinforce Thomas.

Now with a crisis in his center, Rosecrans grabbed another member of his staff, Maj. Frank Bond, and had him write out a simple order to have the next division down move north to fill the gap. The order, written out, was sealed in an envelope and handed to a staff officer who immediately rode from headquarters toward the front.

But the simple order would turn out to be not so simple.

At Poe Field

Earlier in the morning, after he rode his lines, Rosecrans removed his headquarters from Eliza Glenn's and set up on an open knoll about 600 yards south west of here—though it might as well have been 600 miles away for what was about to happen. The battlefield of Chickamauga is probably one of the last places that a Civil War general would have chosen to fight a battle. Ever since ancient times, battles were supposed to be fought in open fields whenever possible. Battlefields like Chickamauga made it next to impossible for a commander to see what was going on and be able to keep control of his forces, where a little mistake might become a huge disaster.

On the morning of September 20, as Rosecrans juggled troops in and out of line and from one part of the field to another, a little mistake was made. General Brannan's division was moved into line here from his position in the north end of Dyer field. Brannan was designated to be a reserve for Thomas, but now was committed to the front lines without letting Thomas know.

Detail of the 14th Ohio's monument showing the intensity of the fighting there.

So, a little later when Thomas called on him for support, Brannan could only send his reserves. The second time Thomas sent for Brannan, he reluctantly agreed to go after consulting with his neighbor, Joseph Reynolds, although they sent word sent to Rosecrans that he was moving out of line and that a gap now existed in his center. Rosecrans, unable to see that Brannan was still in line, was already working on several other movements so he hastily sent what proved to be a poorly worded order to the next division down to fill a gap that did not exist.

⟶ TO STOP 12

Proceed down Poe Road and turn right onto the LaFayette Road. Continue .14 miles to the intersection with Dyer Road and turn right. Proceed .09 miles to the fence line along the edge of the woods on the western edge of Brotherton Field and park along the shoulder of the road.

GPS: N 34.91788 W 85.26261

Maj. Gen. Joseph J. Reynolds commanded a division in the XIV Corps along the south end of Kelly Field. In the final moments of the battle, he panicked and advised a nearby division commander that they should retreat. He then removed his rank insignia and even talked of surrendering before receiving orders from Thomas to withdraw.

Col. Robert Tyler led the Consolidated 15th and 37th Tennessee Infantry into Poe Field on September 20th. "Having approached to within 200 yards, the fire being so destructive, our ranks, having become decimated and receiving no supports, were compelled to retire," he recalled. Tyler was later promoted to brigadier general and became the last Confederate general to be killed in the war, during the battle of West Point, Georgia, in 1865.

Albion Winegar Tourgee (left) was a company officer in the 105th Ohio Infantry. Tourgee was an abolitionist and Radical Republican. After the war, Tourgee became a crusader for civil rights for the African Americans. He achieved national renown for being the lead lawyer for Homer Plessy in the great Civil Rights case *Plessy v. Ferguson*, arguing against the "separate but equal" doctrine.

The Breakthrough

CHAPTER THIRTEEN

SEPTEMBER 20, 1863

During the morning shuffle, James Negley's men had moved out in response to a summons from Thomas; Tom Wood's men had been advanced to the center of the line to fill the resulting gap. Wood's men filed into the line of low works that Negley's men had constructed and sent forward a line of skirmishers into the Brotherton field, where things were quiet for a while—but as the sound of battle roared down from the north, the skirmish line came under fire from Confederates along the wood line on the east side of the LaFayette Road. Some bold Southerners even advanced into the Brotherton farm and occupied it, and from there, they opened a lively fire on Wood's men.

The commander of the skirmish line, Col. Fred Bartleson, decided to clear them out. He ordered two companies of the 100th Illinois to charge. Bartleson's men rushed among the farm buildings and pushed into the woods beyond, driving out the harassing Confederates.

The timing could not have been worse.

As Bartleson began his endeavor, Wood, joined by Alex McCook, heard the galloping of hooves and was soon greeted by Lt. Col. Lyne Starling, the XXI Corps's chief of staff, who handed Wood an envelope. Wood quickly read the order: "Brigadier General Wood, The General Commanding directs that you close up on Reynolds as fast as possible. . . ."

A simple order it would seem, but then it was capped off with three extra words: ". . . and support him."

Close up meant simply to make a sidestep and close any gap; *support* meant to form a line behind. Someone, perhaps Rosecrans himself, had made an error, and that would be disastrous. Wood could do one or the other, but with Brannan still in position, he couldn't simply sidestep, so his only real option was to support Reynolds. That meant he would have to pull out of line in order to get into position behind Reynolds.

The Wilder monument, at 85 feet tall, is the tallest monument on the battlefield.

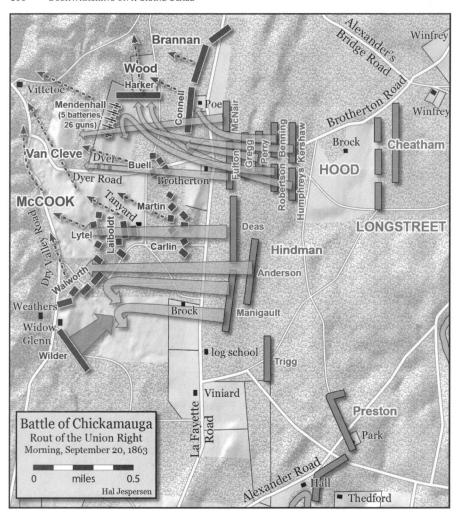

ROUT OF THE UNION RIGHT—The event known as "the Breakthrough" was actually much worse. As Longstreet's wing of the army moved forward, not only did it punch through the yawning gap left by Wood's departure, it also rolled over Jefferson C. Davis's division before smashing into and routing Sheridan's division. The whole right wing of the Union army collapsed in a short time.

The confused general showed the order to McCook who studied it and then offered Wood his view. Rosecrans must know more about the situation than they did, he reasoned, adding that immediate obedience was required. He also offered a reassurance that he would immediately order the next division down from Wood, Jeff Davis's, to fill the gap Wood's departure would create.

McCook immediately mounted and rode south to start Davis in motion even as Wood sent out the orders to get his three brigades moving—opening up a huge gap in the Federal line.

As the last of Wood's brigades filed out of position, a massive wave of Confederates surged out of the woods opposite the gap. By pure blind luck, Longstreet's wing had just been ordered forward—at the very time and at the very place the Federals had created a weak spot.

* * *

Longstreet had spent the morning trying to organize his wing and bring his veterans of the Army of Northern Virginia into the front lines. Two more of brigades from his corps—Brig. Gen. Joseph Kershaw's South Carolinians and Brig. Gen. Benjamin Humphreys' Mississippians—had joined the men of Hood already on the field. As a result of all the subsequent shuffling, Longstreet ordered Stewart's division to move to the north to make room. However, no one bothered to tell Bushrod Johnson, who had been ordered to stay in contact with Stewart. When Johnson moved, he didn't make the space Longstreet desired, which caused Stewart's men to bump in front of Cleburne's men, which in turn created problems for Cleburne when he attacked.

Before Longstreet corrected this mistake, word arrived from Bragg: attack. Longstreet placed Hood in command of the column of divisions that had been created by the pile-up, and a little after 11 a.m., Longstreet's wing of the army moved forward.

They advanced even as Bartleson's small force moved up a slight rise, firing after the retreating Confederate skirmishers. Suddenly, a hail of lead and iron ripped the forest apart around them. Realizing too late that they had blundered into a massive Confederate force, the Illini made a hasty retreat as the Confederate juggernaut pushed toward them. Some of Bartleson's men attempted to make a desperate stand in the Brotherton's cabin and outbuildings, but they were soon captured, Bartleson among them.

The Confederate tide moved onward—right through the gap that Wood had just made, smashing into the final Federal brigade as it tried to follow the rest of the division out of line.

To the south, McCook ordered Davis to shift his two battle-weary brigades into the gap that Wood was making. Davis was beginning to move his troops when the massive Confederate force struck his front. After facing a strong but brief resistance in front, Confederates swarmed around both flanks. Running the risk of being surrounded, the Federals broke and fled westward through the woods with Confederates hot on their heels.

"I heard the pickets fire one round. Immediately afterwards I discovered that they were coming back to the line in haste," said one of Davis's brigade commanders, Brig. Gen. William Carlin.

Col. Frederick A. Bartleson of the 100th Illinois Infantry, a brave if rash officer, was the first to enlist in the Union Army in his hometown of Joilet. A wound at the battle of Shiloh cost him his arm but earned him promotion to colonel of the newly formed 100th Illinois. The 100th Illinois made up the skirmish line in front of the Brotherton Farm. Mere moments before Longstreet's Corps advanced, Bartleson ordered his men forward. Many men of the 100th were captured in the following moments as they tried fruitlessly to stop the juggernaut that rolled over them.

The farmstead of George Brotherton became the epicenter of one of the largest Confederate assaults of the war when Longstreet's veterans surged across the LaFayette Road a little after 11 a.m. on September 20. Confederates swept across the farmstead's fields, then into the woods along the western edge, tearing through the center of the Union line.

Then almost simultaneously, vollys of musketry broke forth in front and on my right flank. There were some large pine trees near me, and the needles from these pines commenced falling in showers to the ground, having been cut loose by the bullets fired at my men. Then the rebel battle flags began to show themselves at the breastworks on my right. There was a hand to hand struggle for a few minutes-then more volleys of musketry on the right and left flanks, as well as in front. The brigade on my left had been flanked and driven away...With attack in front and on both flanks simultaneously, it was impossible for my troops to hold their position. The line melted away . . . .

The making of a huge Confederate success was underway. Longstreet took the opportunity to stop for lunch near the Brotherton cabin as his men pushed onward, then rode on to confer with Bragg. He wouldn't return to the scene of his wing's action until several hours later, entrusting Hood to keep things moving.

*   *   *

The first sign for Rosecrans that something was wrong came when bluecoats burst from the forest into Dyer field across from his headquarters, and then a wall of Confederates burst forth after them. Two full Confederate divisions—the first wave of Longstreet's line—headed straight toward Rosecrans's headquarters.

Rosecrans made his headquarters on a hill that overlooked Dyer Hill. Today, a cannonball pyramid marks the spot (above). A large slab monument to his escort, the 15th Pennsylvania Cavalry, stands nearby. Rosecrans was startled to see his own men falling back pell-mell from the far treeline (left), with Confederates in close pursuit.

"Our lines now emerged from the forest into open ground on the border of long, open fields, over which the enemy were retreating, under cover of several batteries," Johnson recalled. "The scene now presented was unspeakably grand. The resolute and impetuous charge, the rush of our heavy columns sweeping out from the shadow and gloom of the forest into the open fields flooded with sunlight, the glitter of arms, and onward dash of artillery and mounted men, the retreat of the foe, the shouts of the hosts of our army, the dust, the smoke, the noise of firearms-of whistling balls and grape-shot and of bursting shell-made up a scene of unsurpassed grandeur."

Rosecrans and his staff quickly mounted and rode into the throng of terrified soldiers, desperately trying to

From the Confederate position, looking up at what is now known as Lytle's Hill

rally them, but to no avail. With his staff breaking apart, Rosecrans moved with his fleeing men onto the Dry Valley Road and toward McFarland Gap and Chattanooga.

On the southern end of the rise where Rosecrans had established his headquarters, Col. Bernard Laiboldt's brigade of Sheridan's division was formed. McCook galloped up to the German-born Laiboldt and shouted to him that he must advance his brigade immediately to support Davis's division. Laiboldt ordered his command down the slope, still in a column of march. Around them grew the roar of battle and the stream of fugitives from Davis's wrecked division. Leading the column was the 73rd Illinois, known as "The Preacher Regiment" because of the number of ministers in the unit. "We were ordered to fix bayonets and charge across the field and meet the advancing foe, coming eight lines deep toward us," one survivor recalled. "On reaching the edge of pine-grove, orders came for us to halt and fire. This was amid a shower of balls flying from our front, right, and left."

In front of Laiboldt, Brig. Gen. Zachariah Deas's Alabama brigade of Hindman's division halted at the edge of the woods and opened fire. The blast ripped through the blue ranks, sending the 73rd crashing back through the other regiments of the brigade, who in turn collapsed, unable to fire because of the human shield created by their fellow brigade members. The Alabamians howled the Rebel Yell and surged forward. "With an increased shout and rapidity of step, we drove the enemy . . . with great slaughter, and pursued through the open field," recounted Col. Samuel McSpadden of the 19th Alabama.

As catastrophe unfolded for Laiboldt, the rest of Sheridan's division was moving rapidly northward, having received their orders to go to Thomas's assistance. Brigadier General William Lytle's brigade led the way. Lytle, known as the "Poet General" because he'd enjoyed some fame for his "Antony and Cleopatra," was now ordered by Sheridan to immediately deploy his brigade to meet the new oncoming Confederate wave.

Lytle's men rushed from their column into a battle line just as Laiboldt's men streamed through his lines, Confederates hot on their heels. Lytle rode down his lines, hat in hand, shouting encouragement as his men opened fire right into the faces of the onrushing graycoats. Struck at almost point-blank range, the Confederate line wavered, then staggered to a halt—then returned a ragged volley. "Men began to fall on every side and soon all firing blended in one general roar," attested a soldier in the 24th Wisconsin. "Thick and fast came bullets, shot, and shell."

South of Lytle, Col. Luther Bradley's brigade deployed to face Brig. Gen. Patton Anderson's Mississippi brigade. Bradley's brigade was now commanded by Col. Nathan Walworth following Bradley's wounding in Viniard field the previous evening. Walworth deployed his men in a single, long line stretching from Glenn Hill to the foot of the rise where Lytle was deployed. A deep rock-strewn ditch offered some slight protection to part of his line, but the Confederate line extending well beyond Walworth's right flank. For a few desperate minutes, Federals traded blasts of musketry with the Mississippians, who then

From Lytle's Hill, looking down toward the position of the approaching Confederates. The stand of Lytle's Brigade bought some precious minutes for the retreating Union army.

Brig. Gen. William Haines Lytle became the highest-ranking Union officer killed in the battle of Chickamauga.

Walworth's Brigade was afforded strong natural defenses like this rocky ravine, but in the end, the terrain wasn't enough to stem the Confederate tide that came against the Federals.

received support from Brig. Gen. Arthur Manigault's South Carolina and Alabama brigade. Under this added pressure, Walworth's line broke.

The rest of Manigault's brigade continued to advance around Walworth's line toward the Widow Glenn's cabin where a new threat appeared: Federal artillery, which began to hurl shells at them with deadly accuracy. Moving rapidly forward, the Confederates soon staggered under ripping volleys.

Once again, Wilder's brigade appeared to save the day. Wilder's men had been positioned on the extreme right of the army, on a slight ridge to the southwest of the Glenn home. On cue, they rapidly advanced and opened a withering fire with their Spencers into Manigault's Alabama regiments. "They opened upon us with a continuous sheet of fire," shivered Lt. Col. Benjamin F. Sawyer of the 24th Alabama. "We had no time to pause for thought of dread or danger. We were in the very jaws of the monster. We could not retreat. The danger would be greater than to press forward, and onward we pressed . . . it was a fearful alternative and fearfully it cost us. One fourth of my regiment was down . . . . Never before had I, nor since have I, seen such terrible execution in so short a time. It was more than mortal never could bear."

It was indeed more than they could bear, and soon the Alabamans were rushing to the rear.

Wilder moved his men forward toward the LaFayette Road when panic stricken Charles Dana appeared. Dana, a former journalist with the *New York Tribune,* was the assistant secretary of war, traveling with the Army of the Cumberland as a special agent for the War Department. Dana had been sent to poke around Rosecrans's headquarters—in other words, to spy on

The monument for the 24th Wisconsin

Rosecrans, or as Dana later stated, to "observe and report." Some in the Lincoln administration mistrusted Rosecrans, and Dana had been sent to look into things. He failed to be a very good spy, though, as everyone at headquarters knew what he was up to. General Gordon Granger referred to him as "a loathsome pimp," while William Shanks, a reporter traveling with the army, called Dana "a bird of ill omen." Rosecrans and his officers saw him for what he was and treated him as an outsider—not the best attitude given the damage Dana was capable of doing. That damage was now about to come.

Dana told Wilder a tale of complete disaster, that the whole Army of the Cumberland was routed and fleeing from the field and "that Rosecrans was either killed or captured, and the army badly routed, as bad, if not worse than at Bull Run, and that my Brigade was the only portion of the army left intact." Dana then demanded that he be escorted back to Chattanooga and that Wilder to fall back to Chattanooga "as quickly as possible." Thus, one of the hardest-hitting units in the army left the field.

While Wilder pitched into Manigault, Lytle's command continued their uneven contest. Lytle continued to ride along his line, encouraging his men. "Brave Boys . . . Brave Boys!" he called through the

Charles Dana had been a widely read journalist prior to being named assistant secretery of war. His dispatches, friendly to the administration, earned him his government appointment.

The cannonball pyramid to the highest-ranking Union officer killed in the battle, Brig. Gen. William Haines Lytle, was ironically laid low over the years, reduced to a single row of cannonballs because it was used to replace cannonballs on more prominent, visible monuments. In 2013, in observance of the 150th anniversary of the battle, the cannonball stack was returned to its proper height.

leaden storm. One member of the 24th Wisconsin recalled that "the rebels were positively so close to us all this time that we could almost see the whites of their eyes; they crawled up stealthily behind logs, trees and bushes . . . ." A few yards away, a member of the 36th Illinois noted, "We were in a clearing covered with dry grass which was set on fire by the bursting shells. Under the smoke we could see masses of rebels moving toward us and in our front but a few rods distant the enemy's front line lay behind low rail breast works. After holding our position a shirt time we found the rebs to thick for us we were getting sadly mixed up with them, and were ordered to fall back which order was not obeyed by all until several times given."

Battered back, Lytle's presence seemed to be the only thing holding his steadily melting line together as the battle ebbed and surged. Lytle himself had been wounded several times. Now backed up the hillside to the top of the ridge, he suffered a mortal blow: a minie ball smashed into his mouth, and he tumbled from his horse.

Lytle's brigade collapsed, joining Walworth's men fleeing to the rear.

The last fighting force on the Union right ended.

At the Breakthrough

To quote J.R.R. Tolkien in his *Lord of the Rings*: "History became legend, and legend became myth." While there are myths associated with almost every battle, Chickamauga seems to have more than its fair share, with several affecting the most commonly told narrative. One of the most influential centers on Tom Wood and the gap in the Federal line.

As the story goes, on the morning of September 20, Wood was confronted by an angry Rosecrans, who demanded to know why Wood had not moved into line and then proceeded to berate Wood in front of his staff. Later, when Wood received Rosecrans's obviously flawed order, he declared that he has "the fatal order" of the day and maliciously moves out of line, knowingly inviting disaster to befall the army as a way of getting back at his commander.

This tale originated from partisans of General Rosecrans, who tried to clear his name from the black mark Chickamauga left on his otherwise-clean record. These obviously biased accounts became accepted as fact over the years despite public denials from Wood and several others, all of whom backed up their accounts with support from other witnesses. It's worth noting, too, that in the aftermath of Chickamauga when heads were rolling, Wood was not court-martialed or brought up on charges of any sort; he also went on to hold other significant commands through the end of the war. Had Wood acted with malice, there's no way he could've enjoyed the kind of post-battle career that he did.

In this general area, Wood was posted and chatting with McCook when he received the fateful order to move out. Looking toward the Brotherton cabin, a visitor can see that even had the men remained in position, the ground to the east hid Longstreet's column from view until the last minute. Had Wood's men stayed in line, could they have held on? How many rounds could have been fired to break the attack before the Confederates would have been upon them?

The Chickamauga Battlefield has more than 650 monuments and markers on it placed to honor the regiments that fought there. Among the most outstanding, though, is the Wilder Brigade Monument placed to honor the men of Col. John T. Wilder's Lightning Brigade. The monument, funded by the survivors of the brigade, stands 85 feet high and has a stairway that visitors can still take to the top. It was dedicated on September 20, 1899, the battle's thirty-sixth anniversary. It is the most recognizable and iconic monument on the field.

Brig. Gen. Thomas J. Wood became a scapegoat for the Union defeat at Chickamauga in the years after the war, despite strong evidence to the contrary.

Maj. Frank Bond of Rosecrans's staff wrote the order that led to disaster for the army. Whether he miswrote the order or the exhausted Rosecrans stumbled over his words and misstated his intentions is lost to history.

However, their memory overshadows another, that of 23-year-old Eliza Glenn. The Wilder monument now stands upon the site of Glenn's farmstead. Her cabin was only a few feet north of the tower; the hearthstone is visible there today. The Glenn cabin burned to the ground in the final hours of the battle, leaving nothing but ashes for Eliza to find when she returned. Already widowed that year, she had now lost her home and the memories in it. Now, another memory has replaced her story.

During the war, Tennessee was a divided state, providing men to both armies. This monument, opposite, honors the men serving in the 1st and 2nd Tennessee U.S. Cavalry. It's one of the many monuments scattered on the grounds around the Wilder monument.

The Wilder monument (below) offers a beautiful misty-morning view of the Confederate approach (bottom) and the undeveloped expanse of the battlefield park beyond.

The hearthstone of the Glenn farm sits in the ground next to the Wilder monument.

→ **TO STOP 13**

Continue .14 miles on Dyer Road to the intersection with Glenn Kelly Road. Turn right and proceed .20 miles to the edge of North Dyer Field and park in the pull over on the right side.

GPS: N 34.92032 W 85.26439

North Dyer Field

CHAPTER FOURTEEN

SEPTEMBER 20, 1863

As Hindman's division moved against Sheridan, another line of defense confronted Bushrod Johnson's right. Earlier in the morning as Rosecrans began to shift troops and consolidate his lines, Maj. John Mendenhall, the chief of artillery for Crittenden's XXI Corps, began to establish a line of artillery along a ridge on the western edge of North Dyer field—ultimately fielding a line of five batteries, totaling 26 guns.

Now as Johnson's victorious men burst from the woods to the south, two of Wood's beleaguered regiments rushed back to support the gun line. They had a few minutes to prepare as Johnson's right brigade, Brig. Gen. Evander McNair's Arkansasans and North Carolinians, fought their way past Brannan's right. McNair smashed into the Federals and, after a sharp fight, forced them back.

As McNair's men advanced out of the woods, though, the air above them seemed to explode, raining iron shrapnel on their heads. Artillery pummeled the Confederate line, wounding McNair and transferring command to Col. Daniel Coleman, the commander of the 39th North Carolina. Momentarily staggered by the bombardment, Coleman soon had his line moving into the field toward the guns, loading and firing as they advanced. More Confederates joined them—Col. Cyrus Sugg's brigade and Col. William F. Perry's brigade of Hood's division. Into a field of swirling dust and smoke the line surged, closing in on the guns that blasted at them. "The Federal artillerists fought infinitely better than their infantry supports, actually throwing shells and shot with their hands into the faces of our men when they could no longer load their pieces," one Confederate described. "Colonel Coleman was the first to place his hand upon a Federal field piece, and the banner of the 39th North Carolina was the first unfurled above them-cheer after cheer announced the triumph of our gallant men."

The view from one of the spurs of Horseshoe Ridge, looking down across North Dyer field

The view toward Snodgrass Hill from the Confederate perspective across North Dyer field

To their left and right, Sugg and Perry, respectively, had similar results. Altogether, the three brigades captured 15 guns, with the cannon crews either making their escape or falling in a last-ditch struggle for their guns. Among the fallen was Capt. Alanson Stevens of the 26th Pennsylvania Battery, the nephew and ward of Congressman Thaddeus Stevens, recognized as the leader of the Radical Republicans and a fierce opponent of slavery.

Sugg, Perry, and Coleman halted to consolidate their gains while behind them, Robertson's brigade moved out into Dyer field. Robertson's men advanced to the north toward a Union battery deployed on the spur of a ridge. The gunners opened fire on the Texans making their advance—"a veritable hell on earth," one Texan recalled. "Shells, grapeshot, canister, shrapnel and Minie balls were tearing through the air, while dirt, leaves, limbs, and bark were falling and flying all over and around us."

At this point, Tom Wood, who'd been shuffling troops in response to Rosecrans's misinformed order, heard the sound of battle in his rear. He redirected one of his brigades, that of Col. Charles Harker, to investigate. Seeing the disaster developing in the Dyer field, Wood ordered Harker to deploy his command and advance southward, where they quickly clashed with Robertson's Texans. Not expecting to meet such resistance, Robertson's men were surprised by the sudden appearance of Union soldiers advancing toward them. One Texan remarked that "a pretty heavy, though irregular fire was opened on them."

Brig. Gen. Evander McNair commanded a brigade that consisted of one North Carolina Regiment and several from Arkansas.

Harker's men advanced firing, forcing the Texans back. Val Giles of the 4th Texas later noted that it was "the meanest, most unsatisfactory place I struck during the whole war"—a bold statement from a Gettysburg veteran. Having suffered heavily the day before the Texans reached their breaking point and began to stream to the rear.

The sudden appearance of Harker's men also sent Johnson's brigades into a panic, and a virtual stampede started across the Dyer field as men raced for the safety of the woods on the eastern side.

Seeing this, Gen. John Bell Hood rode in among the men of his old brigade. He grabbed the flag of his old regiment, the 4th Texas, and tried to rally his men—all the while still receiving fire from Harker's men, who had now stopped at a fence line along a patch of woods a short distance to the north. Among his milling men, holding the flag and the reins of his horse with his disabled arm, Hood made an excellent target. He soon went down with a gunshot in his right thigh. Any hope of keeping the Texans in the fight now disappeared. They picked up their beloved commander and made their way to the rear.

Confederates now faced a critical moment. Hood had been tasked with leading the attack column, and now someone needed to take over. Bushrod Johnson and Joe Kershaw, the senior commanders on the field, conferred—but neither would agree to let the other assume overall command. Kershaw's men were moving northward toward Harker, and he expressed the belief that the whole force should now move in that direction; meanwhile Johnson believed that pursuit of the fleeing force was the better option.

The site where John Bell Hood was wounded is marked today by a small sign.

After a short but heated discussion, they decided to each pursue their own courses. Kershaw's men continued their advance while Johnson moved to get his command back into action.

As Kershaw's advanced, Harker's men strangely stopped firing at them. Just before leaving Virginia, a large portion of Longstreet's corps had been issued new uniforms made of fine British Kersey, which was blue-gray in color—but it was more blue than gray. At a distance, it appeared to be a dusty blue. Seeing Kershaw's Kersey-clad men, Harker was confused: were they Federals?

As Kershaw's line drew closer, one of Harker's colorbearers stood and began to wave the national colors, hoping to get a response. Finally, just 100 yards away, Kershaw halted his brigade and delivered a devastating volley into the surprised Union soldiers. Harker's men responded with their own ragged fire, but the blow had been too much. Harker decided to make a fighting withdrawal.

Col. Charles G. Harker was one of the young rising stars in the Army of the Cumberland's officer corps. He would die leading an assault at Kennesaw Mountain in 1864.

The South Carolina monument   However, the Federal withdrawal soon turned into a race northward for protection, first through a cornfield and then up a spur of Horseshoe Ridge, known locally as Snodgrass Hill.

At North Dyer Field

Along the ridge to the west of you, Maj. John Mendenhall established the largest concentration of artillery in the battle. Mendenhall had established a similar line of artillery in the battle of Stones River, and that line saved the day, crushing the final Confederate attacking in a hail of iron. Now, Mendenhall hoped that history would repeat itself. Alas, though, history did not prove be so kind this time around. Without infantry support, the line was doomed. Ironically, the largest line of artillery in the fight doesn't have a single cannon commemorating it.

Along the edge of the little thicket of trees, a short walk will take you to the spot where General Hood was wounded. History has not been kind to John Bell Hood. Many historians have sharply criticized his career as a corps commander and as an army commander, blaming him unfairly for losing Atlanta in the fall of 1864 and then later "bleeding" the Army of Tennessee out of existence at the battles of Franklin and Nashville. However, the early afternoon of September 20 might be viewed as the pinnacle of his career. His wounding here struck the Confederates at the worst possible moment, at a time when aggressive and decisive decisions were needed for a complete victory.

The original design of the South Carolina monument included a palm tree in honor of the state symbol. However, the bronze tree acted as a lightning rod and, over the years, was eventually destroyed by storms. It was later replaced by the obelisk that now tops the monument.

⟶ TO STOP 14

Continue 0.5 miles on Glenn Kelly Road until the road splits. Bear left and proceed 0.4 mile to the top of the Hill. Stop in the parking lot at the wayside.

GPS: N34.92774 W 85.26897

Horseshoe Ridge

CHAPTER FIFTEEN
SEPTEMBER 20, 1863

Running roughly east to west, Horseshoe Ridge rises and falls in a series of steep peaks and troughs. Forest-packed ravines and valleys cut into the ridge, and several spurs jut out into the woods and fields. One such spur was known locally as Snodgrass Hill, named for the nearby farm of George Washington Snodgrass.

Seeking protection following their drubbing by Confederates, the remains of Brannan's and Van Cleve's divisions stumbled up Snodgrass Hill and, in small groups, began to form a line. Brannan himself arrived and began to establish a line from the Snodgrass farm southward to the top of a steep hill, where the line then turned westward along the ridge in loop-de-loop fashion, taking advantage of the highest ground and not dropping into the hollows between each hill. (Later, when the park was established, each hill would be designated by a number: Hill One, Hill Two, etc.)

The hill had initially been occupied by the artillery of Negley's divisions along with the infantry brigade of Col. William Sirwell, originally ordered there by Thomas to help support his vulnerable left flank. It now served as a rallying point.

At Brannan's request, Negley dispatched one of his regiments, the 21st Ohio, to form the right flank of the line. The 21st was a large regiment with many of its members armed with the Colt Revolving Rifle, a five-shot repeater. Negley had more than 40 cannon under his charge; now, with only three regiments to guard them, he became increasingly concerned for their safety and finally decided to withdraw them back to Rossville, which he did without consulting anyone.

Brannan's new line, however, was drawing attention, and he was soon joined by Stanley's brigade, moving over from Kelly field. The remains of John Beatty's brigade joined him, too.

A Union monument sits alone atop Stondgrass Hill—a testament to the desperate fighting there.

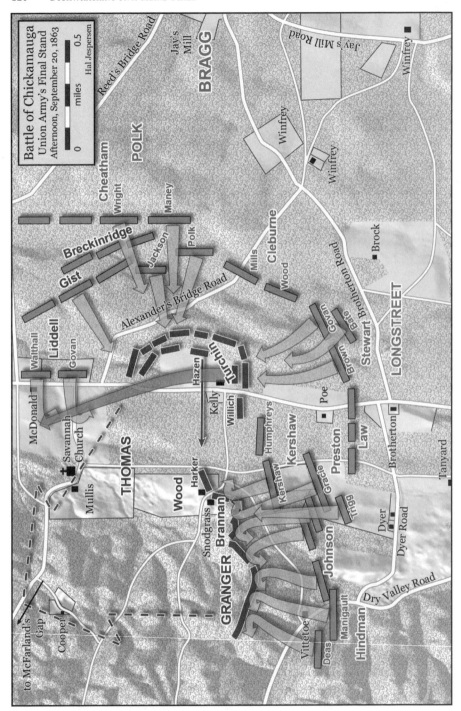

UNION ARMY'S FINAL STAND—Forced back by the collapse of the Union right wing, Brannan's and Wood's divisions took a strong defensive position along the heights of Horseshoe Ridge. They, along with other units that arrived to reinforce the line, withstood repeated but disjointed Confederate assaults throughout the afternoon before receiving orders to withdraw from the field at sundown.

So it was that Brannan was still adjusting his lines when Harker's brigade began to stream into the Snodgrass cornfield with Kershaw's men hot on their heels.

Having reached the hill in the northwest corner of Dyer field, Kershaw's men reformed and, urged forward, came howling down the northern slope into the low ground in front of Hill One. All the while, Union troops atop Hill One poured a vicious fire on them. "Colonel Bland, then Major Hard, commanding Seventh, were killed. Lieutenant Colonel Hoole, of the Eighth was killed," recounted Augustus Dickert of the 3rd South Carolina. "Colonel Gist, commanding the Fifteenth, and Captain Jennings, commanding the Third Battalion were dangerously wounded, while many others of the line officers had fallen, and men were being mown down like grain before a sickle." The Federal position proved too strong for the South Carolinians to take. They recoiled and fell back over the ground they had just advanced across, where they reformed and were once again ordered forward into a leaden hailstorm.

"At first the charging Johnnies, reaching the proper distance and receiving a volley from the regiment, returned the same and then started on the keen jump, expecting to reach us before we could reload," said Lt. William Vance of the 21st Ohio, describing the effect of their fire. "Before they advanced ten paces . . . they would get another volley, and while they were pondering upon

Confederates faced an uphill battle against Federals ensconced on the crest of Hill One.

Brig. Gen. Joseph B. Kershaw

The view from the crest of Hill One, looking down at the direction of the Confederate charges

this circumstance, still a third; then they would scarcely get their backs turned . . . before the fourth would catch them. And on a dead run, the fifth came singing about their ears."

Out on the spur of Snodgrass Hill, Harker's men were also dealing damage. Hidden in the corn, Harker positioned his men along the backside of the ridge so as to not expose them any more than necessary. When Kershaw's men appeared in their front again, Harker's men hit them hard, delivering a volley into them at only a few yards distance, and the Carolinians retreated.

As Kershaw's brigade reformed, Humphrey's Mississippians were ordered forward on Kershaw's right, receiving a heavy fire from artillery posted near the Snodgrass cabin. Humphreys made a half-hearted effort to advance, then stopped and withdrew his men, having decided that the Union position was just too strong. They would play no further part in the fighting that afternoon.

Sugg's and Fulton's brigades reformed, too, and Bushrod Johnson urged them forward, continuing with his last orders from Hood. Johnson's artillery, in particular, helped make life miserable for the retreating Union forces, throwing shells in among the milling mass of men, horses, mules, and wagons.

Hearing the growing roar of Kershaw's fight, Johnson decided to go to the sound of the guns. He moved his men northward, maneuvering them to turn the flank of Brannan's line. His men surged through the forest and

moved up toward the unoccupied ridge just to the west of the 21st Ohio. As they neared the crest, though, a devastating blast of musketry tore through their lines from in front of them, littering the ground with dead and wounded. Federals had materialized out of nowhere.

The Federal troops belonged to Gordon Granger, who had been chomping at the bit all morning to get into action. Granger had listened to the battle for hours with growing anxiety, and finally with the sounds of the fight moving dramatically westward, Granger ordered Brig. Gen. James Steedman to bring his two-brigade division and Dan McCook's brigade from Brig. Gen. James D. Morgan's division, and move with all haste to the battlefield. Granger led the way.

Moving down the LaFayette Road, they soon saw the smoke of battle rising from the distant forest—and then they became part of the hellish panorama as shells began to burst all around them. Bedford Forrest had been assigned to watch the flank and rear of Polk's wing and had amassed a line of artillery on a small ridge just east of the LaFayette Road. When he saw Granger's Federals appear, Forrest opened on them.

Granger's men ducked and dodged as they made their way along. "The first shot struck near my feet, the next burst over our heads," a member of the 113th Ohio claimed, while another said, "[T]he shells made the boys dodge considerable. It was rather amusing to see them. They would be going along on the 'double quick' when a shell would come howling along just above them and

Harker's Brigade formed on the open spur that ran out from Snodgrass Hill. At the time of the battle, the field was planted in corn, and Harker used the crops to conceal his men.

Maj. Gen. Gordon Granger

Brig. Gen. James B. Steedman (above) led the way for Granger's Reserve Corps, arriving on the top of Horseshoe Ridge mere moments before the Confederates and saving Thomas's right flank (top).

down they would go, flat on the ground as it passed, then jump up and trot along . . . ."

The artillery fire forced Granger off the road but did not stop his journey. He continued southward, cross country, leaving Dan McCook behind to face Forrest.

The detour prompted by Forrest proved fortuitous for Granger. As he drew toward the roar of the fighting on Horseshoe Ridge, he happened to head directly toward the spot where he was needed most.

As they neared the ridge, Granger was met by Thomas. Thomas had learned of the disaster to the south and, realizing he was now the senior officer on the field, had ridden over to the scene assume command over the fight. Thomas happily greeted Granger and Steedman and sent their troops off to the west to extend Brannan's beleagured line.

As the new Federals arrivals rushed up the slope of the ridge, the got there just in time to see Bushrod Johnson's men surging toward them only a few yards away. Grangers men opened fire, bringing the Johnson's advance to an abrupt halt. Confederates then broke for the rear, with Federals in pursuit.

Fortunes then shifted again. "[W]e met a sudden check," recalled Lt. William Hamilton of the 22nd Michigan. "A terrific fire was poured into us from front and flank, and in the few minutes we stood there endeavoring to return the fire about one third of our brave fellows went down, killed or wounded. Our lieutenant colonel was shot through the foot and ankle . . . the whole color guard was shot down; four or five of them killed. All this during the ten or fifteen minutes we tried to hold the position."

* * *

The same story was repeated all along the line: see-saw fighting up and down the hillsides.

Finally, Federals received orders to fall back to the crest of the ridge, joining Mitchell's men there. A brief lull settled down as both lines adjusted. A final group of Federal reinforcements arrived: Van Derveer's well-fought brigade. Thomas rode along his position, encouraging his men, while Granger focused his interests on sighting artillery.

Johnson took advantage of the lull to readjust his lines, as well—and prepare for another assault. Confederate reinforcements bolstered his numbers. Thomas Hindman's division moved up the Dry Valley Road, and two of his weary brigades, Dea's and Manigault's, formed to the left of Johnson; Hindman's third, Patton Anderson's Mississippians, filled the gap between Johnson's and Kershaw's divisions. The Mississippians arriving just in time to join Kershaw's third and final attack against Brannan's line, which was repulsed like all of the others.

Hindman now decided it was his turn and ordered his men forward up the steep slopes, with Dea's brigade slightly overlapping Granger's line. "As soon as our heads were visible above the crest of the hill, were met with a terrible volley of grape and canister and Minnie bullets not more than 80 yards distance," said a member of the 50th Alabama. "The men could go no further, death reigned on every side, the grape and canister swept the earth."

The nature of the ground on Horseshoe Ridge aided the Union defenders. The draws or gullies between the distinct hills that made up the ridge served as funnels that crowded the Confederates into a deadly crossfire from the Union defenders.

The monument for the 2nd Minnesota between Hill One and Hill Two

Hindman's brigade broke and fled down the slopes, where their officers rallied them and moved them back up the slope. Reaching the crest again, they were once more swept back—only to return again for a third time and be driven back a third time.

To Dea's right, Manigault met a similar fate. "When we got half way up the hill they opened on us with great fury with grape and canister and with small arms," wrote Lt. Joshua Calloway in the 28th Alabama:

> *But we moved steadily on till we got in about twenty yards of their line where we halted and went regularly to work. Here commenced a scene that beggars description, and God forbid that I should ever have to witness such another. The carnage was awful. Men were shot down all around me. I was indeed in the very midst of death. We fought them this close I suppose about ten minutes when, as if by command, our whole line gave way and away we went down the hill like a gang of sheep.*

Like Dea's men, they were rallied, and again they slugged their way back up the wooded slopes. One of Manigault's staff, C. Irvine Walker wrote of this final struggle along the wooded slopes of Horseshoe Ridge. "Ranks, there were none," he explained. "The men fought from what shelter they could find, and the individual influence and example of the officers was the

FURTHEST ADVANCE OF
MANIGAULT'S BRIGADE
SUNDAY, SEPTEMBER 20TH 1863.
10TH S. C. REGIMENT
CONSOLIDATED
19TH S. C. REGIMENT
COL. JAMES F. PRESSLEY
COMMANDING

only control remaining. Backwards and Forwards, thus went the tide from hill to hill . . . ."

The monument for Manigault's Brigade

Manigault said there was "no more obstinately contested ground anywhere on that day than at this point."

> *The blood of the men seemed to be up, and there was but little flinching . . . for two hours this contest lasted. Our ammunition was expended again and again in many instances, but the men supplied themselves from their dead and wounded comrades, or those of the Yankees, and when it did not suit their own weapons, threw them away and seized their arms . . . . Regiments and companies were inextricably mixed up, and it resembled more a skirmish on a grand scale than the conflict of a line of battle.*

Hindman's men gave their best, but they were just too fought out to have a hope against Granger's fresh troops. Johnson, now joined by Coleman and Anderson, tried once more, but only succeeded in adding to the mounting butcher's bill of casualties.

*   *   *

After finishing his lunch of Nassau bacon and sweet potatoes, Longstreet rode north to meet with Bragg. When they met, Longstreet explained the situation and

The monument marks the farthest point of advance for the North Carolinians along Hill Two, with a monument for the 35th Ohio overlooking it from atop the crest of the hill.

asked for men from Polk's wing, an odd request since he still had Preston's division in reserve. Bragg explained to Longstreet that there were no men left that had any fight left in them. Rejected, Longstreet rode back to his wing, where he learned of Hood's wounding and of the obstinate stand on Horseshoe Ridge.

Longstreet sent orders for Preston to bring his division into the fight, then Old Pete turned to the battlefield himself. When he finally arrived on his front, he quickly realized the situation and set about regaining control of his disjointed command.

Around that same time, in the mid afternoon, Thomas noticed a small group of horseman approaching at a gallop. It was Rosecrans's chief of staff, Gen. James Garfield, accompanied by several other staff officers, who had been ordered to check on Thomas and brief him. Garfield filled Thomas in on the broader situation and the fate of the rest of the army. Rosecrans, at Garfield's insistence, had gone on to Chattanooga to oversee the army's withdrawal and to prepare for the defense of the town, Garfield explained. He offered Thomas no further instructions.

A short time later, another officer arrived, this time with orders. Thomas was to take command of all units still on the field and withdraw them to Rossville, where he was to take up a defensive position around Rossville Gap.

Thomas decided to try to hold on until sundown, believing darkness would aide in his retreat. First, though, he decided it was necessary to abandon his positions around Kelly field so as to not clog the roads with too many retreating forces. He sent word to his division commanders to prepare, then Thomas left Horseshoe Ridge and rode to Kelly field to supervise the withdrawal there.

Brig. Gen. James Garfield, Rosecrans's chief of staff

As Thomas departed, more Confederate reinforcements began to arrive on the opposite side of the field: Brig. Archibald Gracie's largely Alabama

Horseshoe Ridge, circa 1890

brigade. Gracie was an oddity in the Confederate high command. A native New Yorker, he had been living in Mobile before the war working as a cotton factor, a middleman in the cotton business. Gracie's brigade had never seen action before, having spent most of their time in service in garrison duty. Now deploying in front of Brannan's original position, the men stepped off with parade-ground precision. As they passed over the bodies of the dead and wounded of Kershaw's failed attacks, the men finally began to receive fire.

"The moment we appeared on this ridge we were greeted by a ferocious volley of musketry . . . . We had not advanced to the bottom of the ravine before many of our men had fallen, some killed outright, more wounded," one Alabamian wrote. "When I saw how we were being butchered and discovered no ranking officer of the battalion taking charge, I endeavored to get the men to move forward without waiting to fire and reload. I saw General Gracie coming along in the rear of the line on foot. I ran to him and asked what orders he wished me to carry. He said: 'Tell the men for God's sake to go forward.' I then ran along the line repeating the General's order."

The Alabamians surged up the steep hill but couldn't gain the crest as Federals poured volley after volley into them.

They broke for the rear just as another of Preston's brigade advanced to their left, Brig. Gen. John Kelly's command, which swept up a ravine at the junction of Brannan's and Whitaker's line . Kelly's men burst through, gaining a slight foothold, but were unable to go further under a heavy crossfire.

Brig. Gen. Archibald Gracie was a native New Yorker living in Mobile, Alabama, before the war, having married into a local family. Despite strong ties and heritage in New York, he nonetheless fought for the Confederacy. His brigade went into action for the first time assaulting Horseshoe Ridge.

A Tennessee infantryman's cautious advance is captured forever in bronze, recalling the final actions of Bushrod Johnson's men on Horseshoe Ridge.

Gracie was able to rally his men and ordered them forward once more. The 2nd Alabama Battalion, led by their youthful Lt. Col. Boiling Hall, Jr. They "rushed up the slope in the face of furious fire," one of them recounted. "The brave commander was wounded, and the battalion lost nearly a third of the officers and men . . . . The little standard pierced in eighty-three places attests the severity of the fire . . . "

One member of the 19th Illinois, which faced the attack, wrote, "The reports of their guns and our own are blended in a dirge of destruction, and the smoke of musketry . . . . [T]hrough the thick smoke suddenly we see a swarm of men in gray, not in battle line, but an on-coming mass of soldiers bent on burying their bullets in resisting flesh…they are almost on us . . . bayonets lunging in fierce thrust, metallic sparks flying as though from flints; and then the front is a wild scene of fast disappearing masses."

The Alabamians pushed their way over the slight works Federals had thrown up, and in one of the fiercest hand-to-hand encounters of the battle—if not the war— they gained the crest. The Union troops fell back to the opposite crest and took cover, pinning Gracie's men down.

The woods were rapidly darkening as the sun set behind distant Lookout Mountain. Bushrod Johnson, now with Coleman's men, decided to make one more attack. Johnson's attack moved slowly up the ridge, and this time, the blue line that had repelled him gave way. Granger's men had fought as long as they could; now worn out and with little or no ammunition left, they gave up the ground they had fought to hold for so long and retreated into the thickly shadowed woods in their rear.

To their left, Brannan and Wood were taking advantage of a lull after Gracie's withdrawal to pull their men back, as well, and begin the march north toward Rossville.

Not everyone made their escape, though. In the center, three regiments confronted Kelly's foothold: the 89th Ohio, 22nd Michigan, and the 21st Ohio. The trio of regiments didn't receive the word to withdraw and were soon surrounded and captured by the advancing Confederates.

The fight for Horseshoe Ridge and Snodgrass Hill was finally over.

Col. Henry V. Boynton commanded the 35th Ohio. Boynton, along with his brigade commander, Ferdinand Van Derveer, were instrumental in the establishment of the Chickamauga and Chattanooga National Military Park.

At the Breakthrough

The defense of Snodgrass Hill is the most well-known phase of the battle of Chickamauga, though the hill is only a spur of the larger Horseshoe Ridge. This is the site of "the Last Stand of the Army of the Cumberland" on the field, and it's where George Thomas earned his nickname the "Rock of Chickamauga."

Today you will find some of the battlefield's nicer monuments along this ridge. The large number of monuments here gives testimony to the hodge-podge line that was created here as units, fragments of units, and even individual solders became part of a blue wall

The open ridge where Harker's men formed now hosts an interesting array of monuments.

The monument for the 21st Ohio

formed around Brannan's and Wood's lines.

Landscape restoration in this area to return the field to its wartime appearance really gives a feel to the strong

A service road runs between Hill One and Hill Two.

defensive position here, and the small Confederate markers down slope give evidence of the determined assaults. The markers for Joe Kershaw's South Carolinians mark their farthest point of advance against the Union line and can be accessed from several trails that go down the hill toward the gravel service road that is visible below Hill One and Hill Two.

A trail to the west will follow the Union line westward and take you past many fine monuments, notably that of the 21st Ohio, which saved the day on the left flank of this line much like the fabled story of Joshua Chamberlain's 20th Maine at Gettysburg.

To the left of the 21st's monument at the top of Hill Three is the marker for the 2nd South Carolina. Somewhere in the vicinity of this marker, Sgt. Richard Kirkland, acting

as a lieutenant, was killed. As the story goes, Kirkland risked his life during the battle of Fredericksburg to carry water to wounded Union soldiers who fallen in front of the Stone Wall after the Union assaults were repulsed. His act of courage and compassion earned him the nickname "the Angel of Marye's Heights."

Monuments further to the west represent the units of Gordon Granger's Reserves Corps and Bushrod

The monument for Lt. George Landrum sits next to the footpath deep in the woods.

The 121st Ohio monument (left) and the 25th Tennessee monument (right). Both sit at the far end of Horseshoe Ridge.

Johnson's men. One of the nicest monuments to an individual Confederate regiment is the 25th Tennessee's, a unit in Fulton's brigade. The 25th owes their monument to the success of its former colonel, Robert Snowden, who became very wealthy in the post war years.

In this area, you will also find the monument dedicated to all of the Confederate Tennessee Infantry units that fought in the battle. If you continue to the end of the line, you will find the monument for the 121st Ohio Infantry, marking the end of Granger's line. The monument is designed to illustrate how the unit was bent back to the right, simultaneously facing assaults from two directions during one point of the battle.

Well back along the path in the woods that leads along the crests of the hills, hikers will find a large cross erected in honor of Lt. George Landrum. Landrum was an unfortunate member of Rosecrans's staff who accidentally rode into Confederate lines and was killed while trying to deliver a message to Gen. Thomas. The monument was raised by Landrum's family.

Col. Emerson Opdycke, commander of the 125th Ohio Infantry (right). His regiment's monument, along the open ridge near the Snodgrass farm, is capped by one of the most distinctive sculptures on the battlefield: a tiger, reflecting the regiment's nickname, "Opdycke's Tiger's" (above).

⟶ **TO STOP 15**

Proceed 0.5 miles down the hill and bear left at the fork, back onto Glenn Kelly Road. Note that Glenn Kelly Road is one way. Continue 0.6 miles to the intersection with the LaFayette Road and turn left. Continue on 0.12 miles to the park's Tour Stop 1, and once again park in the gravel lot there.

GPS: N 34.93782 W 85.25974

McFarland Gap Road and the Union Withdrawal

CHAPTER SIXTEEN

SEPTEMBER 20, 1863

As Longstreet's wing of the army smashed the Union right, Joe Wheeler's Confederate cavalry went into action further to the south near Lee's and Gordon's Mills.

Wheeler began the day farther south along the banks of Chickamauga Creek near Glass's Mill, facing off against one of Brig. Gen. George Crook's Cavalry brigades. Wheeler dismounted his force, pushed his way across the creek, and drove back Crook's men toward Crawfish Springs in one of the larger cavalry fights in the western theater. It was also one of the most lopsided. Crook faced Wheeler's 5,000 troopers with only around 900 men.

Wheeler could not capitalize on this, though, because of orders from Bragg to move to Lee's and Gordon's Mills and drive back the Union forces there. Wheeler soon after received an order from Longstreet to come to his aide, but he decided to follow Bragg's orders since Bragg was the army commander.

Wheeler pushed across the creek at Lee's and Gordon's Mills and slowly advanced against a small Union cavalry force he found there. Union Brig. Gen. John Mitchell, in charge of that force, realized he could not hope to hold out and ordered his command to withdraw. He also ordered an evacuation of all the wounded that could be moved from the Union field hospitals around Crawfish Springs.

As Thomas's men began to withdraw, Wheeler continued his advance, eventually capturing what was left of the Union army's field hospitals located around Crawfish Springs and in the yard of the Gordon Lee mansion even as darkness settled over northwest Georgia.

* * *

The 10th Wisconsin monument

As the field around Elijah Kelly's farm became filled with retreating Union soldiers, Confederate artillery would ignite his home and burn it to the ground, leaving only his exterior kitchen standing. The Kellys would be forced to live in it following the battle.

To help crack the Union defenses around Kelly field, the Army of Tennessee's Reserve Artillery deployed for action and began to bombard the Union lines.

After the morning attacks around Kelly field, the area had grown quiet except for the occasional sharpshooter—annoying for the most part but occasionally deadly for several Union officers, notably Col. Edward King, one of Reynolds's brigade commanders. This relative inactivity had enabled Thomas to shift troops from Kelly field to aide in the defense of Horseshoe Ridge. Now, as afternoon dissolved into evening, word arrived that Thomas was ordering a withdrawal. Thomas himself arrived in the field just as the south end of the line began to fall back from their battered barricades.

While this was occurring, the Confederates finally began to stir again. A. P. Stewart was the only unit of Longstreet's wing not involved in the assaults on Horseshoe Ridge, and now late in the afternoon he received orders to advance toward the southern end of Kelly field. As he moved, Confederate artillery reserves deployed in the field and began to shell the Federals stationed on the far side of the field.

Simultaneously, Liddell received orders from Hill to try and outflank the Union position from the north. Liddell had grave reservations about the move, but Hill promised him support. Nonetheless, Liddell's two brigades moved alone across the LaFayette Road in front of and south of the McDonald farm.

When Thomas arrived in Kelly ield, he met Turchin's brigade leading the withdrawal from the southern end of the position. Thomas also saw Liddell's men threatening his route of withdrawal. He ordered Turchin to attack at once and clear the field.

Turchin's men burst from the woods along the north

The cannonball pyramid for Col. Edward King sits at the edge of Kelly field.

end of Kelly field and struck the Confederates squarely on the flank, sending them fleeing for safety in the woods to the east. Continuing past the first surprised brigade, Turchin rolled up the next one and seized the high ground around the McDonald farm—clearing the mouth of the McFarland Gap Road and opening the way for Thomas to withdraw the rest of his Kelly field force.

As the Union troops from the south end of Kelly field began to withdraw and the middle brigades began pulling out from the center, Stewart's Little Giants attacked, rushing over the now-abandoned works. A dangerous situation was developing for Thomas: now in the center and northern end of the Federal line, Confederate brigades began to advance once more as the Union men were just beginning to leave their meager fortifications.

With a howl, Confederates charged over works that had halted their earlier advances. They burst into Kelly field in the center, turning an orderly retreat into a mad rush for safety. "Our whole line upon both sides of us, as far as we could see, began to retreat, and then followed the greatest confusion I had ever witnessed," said Warren Johnson of the 33rd Ohio. "We could not hear or understand the command of our officers; some of the boys said they understood the orders were to stand firm, while others said it was to retreat. A terrific fire of shell, solid shot and musketry was pouring upon us, dealing death upon all sides."

Turchin's men cleared the way for a safe Union withdrawal by seizing key high ground.

In the ensuing chaos many soldiers were captured, but the majority made their escape in the growing darkness. Thomas, for better or for worse, had his men out of Kelly field and headed to Rossville even as his lines on Horseshoe Ridge were making their way north, as well.

Col. Edward King, commanding a brigade in Reynold's division, became the final Union brigade commander to fall when he was shot through the head in the battle's final moments in Kelly field.

As Confederate soldiers reached the LaFayette Road, they realized they had won, and a great Rebel Yell echoed through the dark woods. In the distance, Lt. Ambrose Bierce heard it reverberate through the dark wood. "[I]t was taken up successively and passed round to our front, along our right and in behind us again, until it seemed almost to have got to the point whence it started," he described. "It was the ugliest sound that any mortal ever heard—even a mortal exhausted and unnerved by two days of hard fighting, without sleep, without rest, without food and without hope. There was, however, a space somewhere at the back of us across which that horrible yell did not prolong itself; and through that we finally retired in profound silence and dejection, unmolested."

With that yell, the battle of Chickamauga had finally come to an end.

At McFarland Gap Road

The modern service road running off to the west from this point was the wartime McFarland Gap Road. Thousands of Union soldiers made their way from the Kelly field defense line late in the afternoon through the woods just to the south and through the lower part of the McDonald field where Turchin's brigade held the high ground around the McDonald farm, protecting the pass.

A path running parallel to the LaFayette Road will follow part of Turchin's route back to the Visitor Center's lower parking lot. Around the Visitor Center's north side, there are several markers for the units of Turchin's brigade and the cannon they almost captured from Liddell's division.

Sunset on the battlefield near the visitor center (opposite)

The Day After

EPILOGUE

SEPTEMBER 21, 1863

Maj. Gen. George H. Thomas's stand in the final hours of the battle, which earned him the enduring nickname "The Rock of Chickamauga," became legend, and he was the only high-level officer in the Army of the Cumberland to come out of the battle with his reputation intact—indeed, enhanced. Both McCook and Crittenden were relieved of command and court-martialed; though they were not found guilty, they would not return to the Army of the Cumberland. With his eventual promotion to command of the Army of the Cumberland at Chattanooga, Thomas did not enjoy a harmonious relationship with his new superior, U. S. Grant. Indeed, Thomas struggled to escape Grant's preconceived perception that he was slow and unimaginative. Thomas, however, finally destroyed those notions at the battle of Nashville in December of 1864 when "the Rock" crushed the Army of Tennessee in one of the most complete victories of the American Civil War.

Through the night, Thomas's and Grainger's men made their way toward Rossville "in an orderly manner" where they joined the rest of the army bivouacked in and around the village. The next morning, the army was still in good condition, all things considered. "At 8 o'clock next morning were on the line of defense," Lt. Charles Belknap of the 21st Michigan noted. "[N]ot a defeated army so far as the men in the ranks were concerned."

Ammunition and rations were brought up and the men resupplied. Federals moved into defensive positions around Rossville Gap, along Missionary Ridge to the north, and facing south in a line stretching toward Lookout Mountain, then began to build up breastworks, much as they had the day before. Before long, they'd constructed a strong position that would punish the Confederates if they chose to make a strong advance.

Confederates, meanwhile, weren't sure where the Union army had gone. Were they on the next ridge? Were they lying in ambush somewhere? Longstreet sent forward skirmishers, and the cavalry was ordered to scout ahead.

Reports of uncertainty, of units needing rations, and of appalling casualties came in, leaving Bragg in a quandary. Finally, he determined that the Union forces were indeed gone and sent out order for his army to move cautiously forward.

Several engagements flared up then as Forrest's cavalry clashed with Minty's—and then with part of the infantry line near Rossville Gap. Wheeler's cavalry had a rather one-sided victory over Col. Louis Watkins's Kentucky cavalry.

The stout defense of Rossville against Confederate probes began to give Bragg a picture of a far-from-beaten enemy. Then he received a report from Forrest announcing that the Union troops were "evacuating as hard as they can go."

Chattanooga, with Lookout Mountain looming over the town in the background

Bragg again took stock of the situation. He determined that if the Union army was leaving Chattanooga, then he was more than happy to let them go. He had already paid a heavy price for the town and didn't want to lose any more men if he could help it.

Forrest's report was wrong, though. All day, Rosecrans's ambulances and supply wagons made their way into Chattanooga, and he forwarded his wounded on to his railheads at Stevenson, but that was his only rearward movement. He had no mind to retreat; indeed, he had determined to hold the town until the last.

However, unlike his men, Rosecrans was mentally broken by the defeat at Chickamauga. That evening, he ordered his forces back into the old Confederate-made fortifications around Chattanooga, giving up the high ground of Missionary Ridge and Lookout Mountain— setting the stage for the Confederate siege that would follow.

Thomas (second from left) and his staff atop Lookout Mountain

Although Bragg won the battle of Chickamauga, he had lost the city. For many of the soldiers in the Army of the Cumberland, a look at the big picture didn't look so bad. "[A]s it turns out," said Harold Bartlett of the 1st Michigan Light Artillery, giving voice to the attitude of many of his peers, "we claim a great victory."

Chattanooga's ultimate fate, though, was not necessarily so rosey. The future of the city would be determined by another campaign, more battles, and more casualties—and a leading character from a different stage of the western theater named Ulysses S. Grant.

*   *   *

In the months after Chickamauga, fate was unfair to William Rosecrans. He had never lost a battle until then and, even in defeat, he still managed to retain control of the city that President Lincoln had called as important as Richmond. In the days that followed the battle, and as Bragg laid siege to the town, Rosecrans began to develop more plans, but he would not have a chance to implement them. Lincoln promoted Ulysses S. Grant to take command of the theater. Grant, a bitter enemy of Rosecrans, relieved him of command and replaced him with George Thomas. Rosecrans was ordered to the Department of Missouri, where he served for a time before resigning.

The Army of the Cumberland in front of Chattanooga

Bragg found himself under similar siege. In the wake of his victory at Chickamauga, a number of Bragg's subordinates signed a mutinous petition to have him relieved of command. Generals Buckner, Preston, Gracie, D. H. Hill, John C. Brown, Bushrod Johnson, Stovall, Lucius Polk, James A. Smith, Patrick Cleburne, and James Longstreet, along with Col. Randall Gibson, signed the document and forwarded it to Richmond. While this was a small percentage of the commanders present with the army, the petition's arrival was enough to prompt President Davis to visit Chattanooga to investigate the matter. In the end, he stood by Bragg. However, Bragg's tenure as commander of the Army of Tennessee would end before the end of the year when he resigned a few days after his defeat in the battles for Chattanooga; Gen. Joseph Johnston eventually replaced him. Bragg, meanwhile, was reassigned to become Davis's military advisor, a post that had been previously held by Robert E. Lee.

Longstreet's Move

APPENDIX A

"Never before were so many troops moved over such worn-out railways, none first-class from the beginning," recalled one Confederate, referring to one of the most incredible feats accomplished by the Confederacy during the war. "Never before were such crazy cars—passenger, baggage, mail, coal, box, platform, all and every sort wabbling on the jumping strap-iron—used for hauling good soldiers. But we got there nevertheless."

Moxley Sorrel, Gen. James Longstreet's chief of staff, was describing the movement of the battle-scarred veterans of Longstreet's Corps, of General Robert E. Lee's vaunted Army of Northern Virginia, to reinforce Bragg. The feat was a massive undertaking that taxed the Confederacy's rail resources to the maximum extreme and ultimately involved 16 different rail lines and several different routes to get the men from central Virginia to northern Georgia.

Longstreet had campaigned several times for transfer to the greener pastures of the western theater. He dreamed of an opportunity to escape Lee's shadow and maybe even get command of his own army. To this end, he looked to the misfortunes of the Confederacy in the western theater and saw himself as the would-be savior.

He finally got his chance in September of 1863. Following the traumatic summer debacles—the Tullahoma Campaign, the fall of Vicksburg, and Lee's defeat at Gettysburg—the Confederacy could ill-afford the loss of the "gateway" to the deep south, Chattanooga. President Jefferson Davis had already ordered several thousand reinforcements to Bragg's army, but in early September, with Rosecrans moving on the city and with Knoxville being threatened by Maj. Gen. Ambrose Burnside, Davis knew he could not afford another disaster. Davis gave Longstreet the opportunity the burly Georgian so desperately wanted: Longstreet was ordered to Chattanooga. With him, he was to take the divisions of Maj. Gens. LaFayette McLaws and John Bell Hood—being temporarily commanded by Brig. Gen. Evander Law since Hood's wounding at Gettysburg. He was also to take the brigade of Brig. Gen. Micah Jenkins, and the artillery battalion of Col. Edward Porter Alexander.

Longstreet's men received their orders in their camps around Orange Court House and along the Rapidan. Most of them began to mobilize in the early morning hours of September 8, boarding trains to make the journey to Richmond—"a lengthy process," one participant recalled. The vanguard arrived in the capital

Lt. Gen. Jame Longstreet's men came from the east on the heels of the battle of Gettysburg (where Longstreet's statue, left, now stands). Their part in the fight at Chickamauga meant they participated in the two biggest battles of the war.

When he came west, Longstreet brought with him some of his corps' top talent (clockwise, from top left): artillery genius Col. E. Porter Alexander; rising-star Brig. Gen. Micah Jenkins; stalwart Maj. Gen. LaFayette McLaws; and Chief of Staff Moxley Sorrel.

the following morning where they presented quite a scene in their new uniforms. During the previous few weeks, a large issue of new uniforms had been made to replace the ragged and filthy uniforms that Longstreet's men had worn through the Gettysburg campaign. The new uniforms consisted of royal blue trousers and a jacket made of blue-gray British-imported wool kersey.

The men took advantage of the brief time they had in the capital to hit the bars and enjoy the sights the city offered. While there, the men of Hood's division met their commander, who was recovering from the arm wound he received at Gettysburg. Many of them asked Hood to accompany them to the west, and their commander agreed, even though he hadn't fully recovered.

That evening, as Longstreet's men continued to disembark in the city, the early arrivers began to board trains to take them further south. Troops would continue to arrive and depart until September 16. The men climbed into and onto the tops of boxcars and men punched holes in the sides until only the frame and roof remained; others boarded flat cars and any other type of car that could carry troops.

Over the next several days, the troops continued to

make their way south. In the Carolinas, the scenes that greeted them were reminiscent of early days of the war. Cheering crowds greeted them at every station "waving handkerchiefs and flags," remembered Augustus Dickert of the 3rd South Carolina of Kershaw's brigade. The soldiers cheered the crowds in return, and a festive atmosphere grew among them.

The trip wasn't without incident, though. As Benning's Georgia brigade stopped in Raleigh, North Carolina, some of the Georgians decided they had a score to settle. Newspaperman William Woods Holden was an outspoken critic of Jefferson Davis and North Carolina Governor Zebulon Vance, using his newspaper, the *North Carolina Standard*, as his platform. The Georgians ransacked the newspaper's office and destroyed the printing press. A riot almost ensued before the Georgians made their way back to their train.

As the trains continued their way south, some towns set up feasts. One of Benning's Georgians, W. R. Houghton of the 2nd Georgia Infantry, remembered one in particular. "Figs, water-melons, cakes, pies, apples, everything one could desire, were thrust on us in profusion," he wrote. Some soldiers also took advantage of the cheering crowds to snatch high-quality hats from some men's heads as they rode past, while others received cards with the names and mailing addresses of young single women looking for a soldier beau.

After a trip of nearly 900 miles that utilized 16 different rail lines, the first of Longstreet's troops—

"Never before were so many troops moved over such worn-out railways."
— G. Moxley Sorrel

Hood's Texas brigade—arrived at the Catoosa platform a couple of miles from Ringgold on September 17. The rest of the corps continued to arrive in bits and pieces over the next several days. Hood's Division would fight at Chickamauga on September 19 and 20, while part of Mclaws's division—Kershaw's South Carolina and Humphrey's Mississippi brigades—arrived in time to fight on September 20. Longstreet himself did not arrive on the field until well into the night on September 19. Longstreet's Corps contributed a little more than 6,700 men to Bragg's army for the battle, roughly half of what had boarded on the trains. The rest arrived in the following days.

Although Longstreet and his men made a tremendous impact upon their arrival in the west, things quickly changed as the Confederates laid siege to Chattanooga. Longstreet became embroiled in the political quagmire of the high command of the Army of Tennessee and other problems boiled up within his own corps. After Hood's wounding, Longstreet sought to place Brig. Gen. Micah Jenkins, a favorite of his, into command of Hood's division, removing Brig. Gen. Evander Law, who was the senior brigadier in the division and popular with the command. What followed cast a black eye on Longstreet as he blackballed Law to get Jenkins into the command.

Then, in early November, the Union Army of the Ohio, commanded by Maj. Gen. Ambrose Burnside, began threatening Bragg from Knoxville. It was decided that Longstreet would be given an independent command and sent to deal with his fellow Easterner. The Knoxville Campaign was an utter disaster, however, as Longstreet delayed and blundered and, against the advice of several of his commanders, ended up launching an attack against the heavy fortifications that ringed the city. In the aftermath, Longstreet cast blame on others, and he removed and arrested several of his commanders, notably generals LaFayette McLaw and Evander Law. What had started as

Among the soldiers in Longstreet's Corps was Sgt. Richard Kirkland of the 2nd South Carolina, whose acts of mercy toward wounded Federals during the 1862 battle of Fredericksburg had earned him the nickname "The Angel of Marye's Heights." By September 20, 1863—some nine months later—Kirkland found himself storming the heights of Snodgrass Hill at Chickamauga.
He was killed during the assaults.
A monument to Kirkland's regiment on Hill Three marks the farthest advance of the unit and the vicinity of Kirkland's death (right).

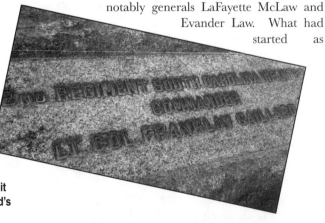

a great opportunity for Longstreet and his command ended in great failure.

Much has been made of the transfer of Longstreet's Corps to reinforce Bragg, but it should be noted that they were not the only reinforcements. In the days and weeks leading up to the battle, many more troops had been sent to Bragg from other parts of the western theater—notably the brigades of Walker's division and Buckner's command from the Department of East Tennessee, who together totaled in the neighborhood of 8,300 men. Still, the arrival of the veteran troops from Lee's already-fabled army and veteran commanders, like Hood, definitely benefited the Confederates in the fight and contributed to the legacy of Longstreet's Corps as a fighting unit.

However, to many of the men of the Army of Tennessee, Longstreet's men did not especially impress—especially because of their attitude. A gunner in Stanford's Mississippi Battery, noticing the appearance of Longstreet's men, suggested that they were more style than substance. "If this command was a specimen of Lee's troops," he said, "they are certainly superior to the troops of the Army of Tennessee, in dress."

Lot Young, an officer with the Orphan Brigade, summed it up best: "Longstreet's Virginians had come out to show the Western army how to fight, and they were now learning that Rosecrans' Western veterans could give instructions in the art of war as well."

Civilians at Chickamauga
APPENDIX B

The farm fields around Chickamauga Creek became killing fields in the late summer days of 1863. For the 22 families that called the area home, the battle of Chickamauga was a life-changing event. The majority of the families were farmers or employed in occupations needed in a yeoman farming community. For the most part, they lived in rustic log cabins, and they cut their crop fields—corn and wheat mostly—out of the tangled forest that surrounded their farms. The farmers tended to be yeoman—subsistence-level farmers or in some cases tenants, not even owning the land that they worked upon. Families were large, consisting of many children who were all expected to work the farm. Any education they received was worked in around the planting and harvesting seasons. The families tended to be fiercely independent and masters of their own small worlds, where the patriarch ruled supreme—a common trait throughout the Antebellum South.

The families of Chickamauga all offered their own unique story and should be considered the forgotten victims of the battle.

GEORGE AND MARY BROTHERTON

George and Mary Brotherton were recent arrivals to the area, constructing their farmstead in 1860 as the war clouds formed. George was a cobbler by trade and relied on the labor of his three eldest sons to work the farm as he traveled through the community looking for work, while Mary and his three daughters and two younger sons worked around the household. The three eldest sons along, with George's son-in-law, Larkin Poe, enlisted in the Confederate army, but all four eventually deserted. When the battle began, the family fled, staying away until the battle ended. One of the Brotherton girls, Adaline, returned afterwards to find

The Brotherton farm, circa 1890 (above); the Snodgrass farm today (opposite)

The Brotherton farm today

that the family's milk cows had survived, but also found that the house had been torn to pieces. With dead and wounded union soldiers in the yard, the cabin looked like a slaughter pen. The family eventually returned and buried nine Union soldiers in their yard. They tried to start anew, though the strain was too much for George, who passed away later in the year.

ELIZA GLENN

John Glenn built his home a short distance from his family's farm, intending to start his own life with his young bride, Eliza. They built their home and began

a family of their own, starting with a son, but the war drums began to draw young men into military service. John resisted, trying to run his farm and take care of his family, but he was conscripted into Confederate service in February of 1863. He kissed his wife and his son goodbye and left to join his regiment. Two months

The Glenn farm burned down during the battle. The hearthstone remains visible.

later he was dead—not killed on the battlefield but dead from disease at a hospital in Mobile, Alabama, where he was buried. Eliza, at the age of 23, found herself a widow with few prospects. To assist her, her parents, the Camps, sent one of their slaves to help her run the farm. On September 19, Eliza found an uninvited guest at her doorstep: Union Gen. William Rosecrans. Rosecrans used the Glenn home as his headquarters throughout September 19 and early into the morning of September 20. On his departure, he advised the young widow to leave before the battle renewed. Eliza took her son and slave and went to her parents'. During the fighting on September 20, Confederate artillery fire set the cabin ablaze and destroyed it. Just like the happy life that John Glenn had tried to provide Eliza, it was all ashes by the end of September 20. Eliza never returned, and today only the hearthstone remains as a sign—and even it lies mostly unobserved near a plaque marking the site of the home.

JAMES REED

James and Sarah Reed had a respectable little farm near the banks of the Chickmauga Creek by the time the war began. Soon thereafter, all three of their sons joined other local boys in enlisting in Company D, of the 1st Confederate Infantry. Joining them was John Ingraham, a laborer on the farm who was more like family because, as an orphan, he'd been brought up with the brothers. As the battle began on September 18, the family fled—fortunate for them because the home soon came under fire as the armies struggled for control of the nearby bridge that bore the family's name. The following day, tragedy struck when Ingraham was killed. The brothers buried their friend on the field near the spot where he

Sgt. John Ingraham is the only soldier known to still be buried on the battlefield. Ingraham worked as a farm hand for the Reed family before the war and enlisted with the Reed brothers, and many other local boys, in the 1st Confederate Infantry. Ingraham fell not far from where he is now buried along Alexander's Bridge Road.

fell and a little over a mile from their home; he remains there today, being the only soldier known to still rest on the battlefield. The Reed brothers survived the war and returned to their home at war's end and continued to live in the area until their deaths years later.

GEORGE WASHINGTON SNODGRASS

Snodgrass is arguably the most famous family name on the Chickamauga battlefield. George Snodgrass was 53 years old at the time of the battle and lived with his

third wife, Elizabeth, and seven of his children. One son, Charles, served in the Confederate army along with several other local men; however, like many other local boys, his devotion to the Confederacy wasn't very strong, and he deserted in the summer of 1863. George made his livelihood by farming and

The Snodgrass home, circa 1890

was evidently fairly successful, having a respectable-sized farm and home along with respectable real and personal estate. When the sounds of battle were heard to the east on September 18 and 19, George refused to leave his home until stray bullets began to strike the house and the surrounding area—only then did the family flee to refuge in a nearby ravine, where several other families joined them. When the fighting finally ended, George returned to find his home a nightmarish scene: bullet and cannon damage had torn up the house and out buildings, the walls and floor of the home were covered in blood. The house was still being used as a hospital, too. The family would refugee around the area for a year, only returning to collect bullets and shrapnel that they were able to sell for scrap in Chattanooga. After the war, the family returned and rebuilt, though the farm never fully recovered from the damage the battle brought.

Interior of the Snodgrass home today

The families who lived on what became the Chickamauga battlefield were hearty folk who had to literally cut their fields out of the forest and endure cold winters and hot, dry summers like those of 1863.

TABLER CHRISTIAN VINIARD

Tabler and Anna Viniard, along with their six children, were new arrivals to the area when the war began. In 1862, his son enlisted in the Confederate army even as the rest of the family struggled to establish their farm along the LaFayette Road. When the battle arrived on their property, the Viniards were already gone, having left when the first shots were heard. As the havoc of battle raged around their farm, the devastation in the fields was horrible, grinding the family's corn crop into the bloody soil and replacing it with a crop of the dead. All of this was evidently too much for Tabler; after the Union army reoccupied the area in 1864, he enlisted with the Federals. The unit Tabler enlisted in, the 1st Georgia U.S., never filled up to take to the field, but Tabler was still a casualty. He fell ill in August and soon died. James, his Confederate son, never made it home either. Captured in the battle of Resaca, Georgia, in May of 1864, James died in a prisoner of war camp in Alton, Illinois.

Chickamauga in Memory
APPENDIX C

It can rightfully be said that I was born on the Chickamauga battlefield. Indeed, the hospital in which I was born sports two cannon and one of the battlefield's unit tablets at its front entrance, being on part of the battlefield that was not preserved within the confines of the Chickamauga and Chattanooga National Military Park.

Chickamauga, however, is still a big place—more than 5,000 acres with more than 660 monuments, markers, and tablets to tell you what unit did this and that. Going out any trail back away from the main roads on a late summer afternoon can transport you back in time and give you an idea of the chaos that reigned supreme on those long ago September days. You can appreciate why the veterans of this battle finally came together and worked to have this set aside as the nation's first national military park in 1890 for "the purposes of marking for historical and professional military study the fields of some of the most remarkable maneuvers and most brilliant fighting in the war of the rebellion."

The park was born in the height of the nation's great "coming back together" as the aging veterans moved to focus on what they had in common instead of what had divided them. On the heights of Lookout Mountain stands the New York Peace Monument, topped by a bronze sculpture of a Union and Confederate soldier shaking hands. It's a heartwarming thing.

However, like a lot of our beloved stories about American history, it's not really true. It was hard for some on both sides to bury the

The author as a toddler (above), visiting the Brotherton farm with his mother during one of many childhood visits to Chickamauga. The 79th Pennsylvania monument (opposite) captures the triumph and tragedy of the battle.

hatchet. Especially troubling to Union veterans was the expense of throwing away what had brought the war on to begin with—slavery—and what the meaningful legacy of the war was—emancipation—

Sunset through the Florida state monument

despite the fact that most Union soldiers had marched off to war "to preserve the Union." Exposure to the institution of slavery as they campaigned into the Deep South helped them determine that emancipation gave their suffering a higher meaning, but their sacrifice was lost with the failure of Reconstruction and the return of White rule and establishment of Jim Crow laws that practically re-enslaved African Americans living in the South. Now faced with how their legacy was going to be viewed, and faced with a need for the country to become united, the meaninglessness of their sacrifices proved a difficult pill to swallow for many.

When the speeches began for the dedication of the park, most followed the reunionist tone—what one Chickamauga veteran, former Brig. Gen. William Walthall, called "blue gray gush."

It is rather ironic that over the years Chickamauga became less and less well known, and now it receives little attention, despite being the second-bloodiest battle of the entire war. Usually, it's that type of superlative that generally hooks the interest of many Civil War buffs. Instead, when the battle does get a mention, it tends to be grouped with the battles of Chattanooga, fought more than two months later.

In recent years, that has started to change, and even as I write this, two major works are underway on the battle that will help reestablish its prominence in Civil War history. Additionally, on the eve of the sesquicentennial, the park was rated as one of the top-twelve and top-ten Civil War sites to visit by CNN and *National Geographic*, respectively.

Of course it's always been a top site for me—from those countless visits as a child, then when I worked there during the summer months while I was in college doing living history programs, and then finally when I landed a job as a ranger. Chickamauga seems to have always been part of my life.

The soldiers wanted to be remembered, and I like to think that I do my part in telling their stories, constantly researching and finding new ones to share—from those of the men of the 19th Illinois defending Hill Number One above the Snodgrass Cabin to those of the Orphan

Georgia monuments on the battlefield differentiate a unit's branch of service with distinctive icons (at bottom, from left to right): crossed cannon tubes for artillery, a horseshoe for cavalry, and a cartridge box for infantry. The three branches of service are also highlighted on the state's monument in Poe Field (above).

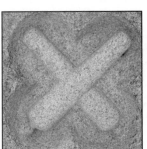

The "Riderless Horse" monument of the 1st Wisconsin Cavalry is one of the most poignant on the battlefield, evoking the terror and loss suffered by many.

The author at a park-sponsored living history event in the early 1990s.

Col. William Stoughton (opposite), now missing his sword and hands due to vandalism, keeps an eternal vigil over the position his men so gallantly defended above the Snodgrass cabin.

Brigade charging into the hellish fire of Thomas's men around Kelly Field. They were young men with their lives ahead of them, with hopes, dreams, desires, and talent—and for many of them, it was all snuffed out here. As a result, much was lost to all of us on these fields. I like to think that I have done a little to keep their memory alive and show that they were flesh and blood, not granite and bronze like the fig-ures on the monuments.

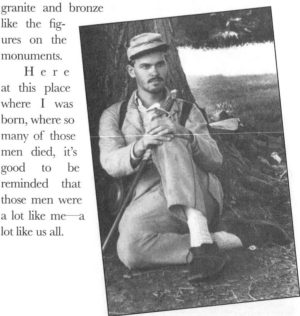

 Here at this place where I was born, where so many of those men died, it's good to be reminded that those men were a lot like me—a lot like us all.

THE BATTLE OF CHICKAMAUGA

ARMY OF THE CUMBERLAND Maj. Gen. William Starke Rosecrans
General Headquarters
1st Battalion Ohio Sharpshooters · 10th Ohio Infantry · 15th Pennsylvania Cavalry

FOURTEENTH CORPS Maj. Gen. George H. Thomas
Provost Guard *9th Michigan Infantry*
Escort *1st Ohio Cavalry, Company I*

FIRST DIVISION Brig. Gen. Absalom Baird
First Brigade Col. Benjamin Scribner
38th Indiana · 2nd Ohio · 33rd Ohio · 94th Ohio · 10th Wisconsin · 1st Michigan, Battery A

Second Brigade Brig. Gen. John C. Starkweather
24th Illinois · 79th Pennsylvania · 1st Wisconsin · 21st Wisconsin · 4th Indiana Light Artillery

Third Brigade Brig. Gen. John H. King
15th United States · 16th United States · 18th United States · 19th United States
5th United States, Battery H

SECOND DIVISION Maj. Gen. James Negley
First Brigade Brig. Gen. John Beatty
104th Illinois · 42nd Indiana · 88th Indiana · 15th Kentucky · Bridge's Illinois Battery

Second Brigade Col. Timothy Stanley; Col. William Stoughton
19th Illinois · 11th Michigan · 18th Ohio · 1st Ohio, Battery M

Third Brigade Col. William Sirwell
37th Indiana · 21st Ohio · 74th Ohio · 78th Pennsylvania · 1st Ohio, Battery G

THIRD DIVISION Brig. Gen. John M. Brannan
First Brigade Col. John M. Connell
82nd Indiana · 17th Ohio · 31st Ohio · 38th Ohio · 1st Michigan, Battery D

Second Brigade Col. John M. Croxton; Col. Charles W. Chapman; Col. William H. Hays
10th Indiana · 74th Indiana · 4th Kentucky · 10th Kentucky · 14th Ohio · 1st Ohio, Battery C

Third Brigade Col. Ferdinand Van Derveer
87th Indiana · 2nd Minnesota · 9th Ohio · 35th Ohio · 4th United States, Battery I

FOURTH DIVISION Maj. Gen. Joseph J. Reynolds
First Brigade Col. John T. Wilder
*17th Indiana · 72nd Indiana · 123rd Illinois · 92nd Illinois · 98th Illinois
18th Indiana Battery*

Second Brigade Col. Edward A. King; Col. Milton S. Robinson
68th Indiana · 75th Indiana · 101st Indiana · 105th Ohio · 19th Indiana Battery

Third Brigade Brig. Gen. John B. Turchin
18th Kentucky · 11th Ohio · 36th Ohio · 92nd Ohio · 21st Indiana Battery

TWENTIETH CORPS Maj. Gen. Alexander McDowell McCook
Provost Guard *81st Indiana, Company H*
Escort *2nd Kentucky Cavalry, Company I*

FIRST DIVISION Brig. Gen. Jefferson C. Davis
First Brigade Col. Sidney Post
59th Illinois · 74th Illinois · 75th Illinois · 5th Wisconsin Battery

Second Brigade Brig. Gen. William P. Carlin
21st Illinois · 38th Illinois · 81st Indiana · 101st Ohio · 2nd Minnesota Batttery

Third Brigade Col. Hans Heg; Col. John A. Martin
8th Kansas · 15th Wisconsin · 35th Illinois · 25th Illinois · 8th Wisconsin Battery

SECOND DIVISION Brig. Gen. Richard W. Johnson
First Brigade Brig. Gen. August Willich
32nd Indiana · 15th Ohio · 89th Illinois · 49th Ohio · 39th Indiana · 1st Ohio, Battery A

Second Brigade Col. Joseph B. Dodge
79th Illinois · 29th Indiana · 30th Indiana · 77th Pennsylvania · 20th Ohio Battery

Third Brigade Col. Philemon P. Baldwin
6th Indiana · 5th Kentucky · 1st Ohio · 93rd Ohio · 5th Indiana Battery

THIRD DIVISION Maj. Gen. Phillip H. Sheridan
1st Brigade Brig. Gen. William H. Lytle
21st Michigan · 24th Wisconsin · 88th Illinois · 36th Illinois · 11th Indiana Battery

2nd Brigade Col. Bernard Liaboldt
2nd Missouri · 15th Missouri · 44th Illinois · 73rd Illinois · 1st Missouri Battery G

3rd Brigade Col. Luther P. Bradley; Col. Nathan Walworth
22nd Illinois · 27th Illinois · 42nd Illinois · 51st Illinois · 1st Illinois Battery C

TWENTY-FIRST CORPS Maj. Gen. Thomas L. Crittenden
Escort *15th Illinois Cavalry, Company K*
FIRST DIVISION Brig. Gen. Thomas J. Wood
First Brigade Col. George Buell
100th Illinois · 58th Indiana · 13th Michigan · 26th Ohio · 8th Indiana Battery

Second Brigade Brig. Gen. George D. Wagner
15th Indiana · 40th Indiana · 57th Indiana · 97th Ohio · 10th Indiana Battery

Third Brigade Col. Charles G. Harker
125th Ohio · 64th Ohio · 65th Ohio · 3rd Kentucky · 6th Ohio Battery

SECOND DIVISION Maj. Gen. John M. Palmer
First Brigade Brig. Gen. Charles Cruft
31st Indiana · 1st Kentucky · 2nd Kentucky · 90th Ohio · 1st Ohio, Battery B

Second Brigade Brig. Gen. William B. Hazen
9th Indiana · 6th Kentucky · 41st Ohio · 124th Ohio · 1st Ohio, Battery F

Third Brigade Col. William Groce
84th Illinois · 36th Indiana · 23rd Kentucky · 6th Ohio · 4th United States, Battery H
4th United States, Battery M

THIRD DIVISION Brig. Gen. Horatio P. Van Cleve
First Brigade Brig. Gen. Samuel Beatty
79th Indiana · 9th Kentucky · 17th Kentucky · 19th Ohio · 7th Indiana Battery

Second Brigade Col. George F. Dick
44th Indiana · 86th Indiana · 13th Ohio · 59th Ohio · 26th Pennsylvania Independent Battery

Third Brigade Col. Sidney M. Barnes
35th Indiana · 8th Kentucky · 51st Ohio · 99th Ohio · 3rd Wisconsin Battery

CAVALRY CORPS Brig. Gen. Robert B. Mitchell
FIRST DIVISION Col. Edward M. McCook
First Brigade Col. Archibald Campbell
1st Tennessee · 2nd Michigan · 9th Pennsylvania

Second Brigade Col. David M. Ray
2nd Indiana · 4th Indiana · 2nd Tennessee · 1st Wisconsin · 1st Ohio, Battery D

Third Brigade Col. Louis D. Watkins
4th Kentucky · 5th Kentucky · 6th Kentucky

SECOND DIVISION Brig. Gen. George Crook

First Brigade Col. Robert H.G. Minty
*3rd Indiana Battalion · 4th Michigan · 7th Pennsylvania Cavalry 4th United States
Chicago Board of Trade Battery (Two Guns)*

Second Brigade Col. Eli Long
2nd Kentucky · 1st Ohio · 3rd Ohio · 4th Ohio · Chicago Board of Trade Battery (Two Guns)

RESERVE CORPS Maj. Gen. Gordon Granger
FIRST DIVISION Brig. Gen. James B. Steedman
First Brigade Brig. Gen. Walter C. Whitaker
*96th Illinois · 115th Illinois · 84th Indiana · 22nd Michigan · 40th Ohio · 89th Ohio
18th Ohio Battery*

Second Brigade Col. John G. Mitchell
78th Illinois · 98th Ohio · 113th Ohio · 121st Ohio · 1st Illinois Light Artillery, Battery M

SECOND DIVISION Brig. Gen. James D. Morgan
Second Brigade Col. Daniel McCook
*85th Illinois · 86th Illinois · 125th Illinois · 52nd Ohio · 69th Ohio ·
2nd Illinois Light Artillery, Battery I*

*   *   *

ARMY OF TENNESSEE Gen. Braxton Bragg
General Headquarters *Dreux's Company, Louisiana Cavalry*
3rd Alabama Cavalry, Company K · 1st Louisiana Regulars, Company C

POLK'S CORPS Lt. Gen. Leonidas Polk
Escort *Greenleaf's Company, Louisiana Cavalry*

CHEATHAM'S DIVISION Maj. Gen. Benjamin Franklin Cheatham
Jackson's Brigade Brig. Gen. John K. Jackson
*1st Confederate · 5th Georgia · 5th Mississippi · 8th Mississippi · 2nd Georgia Sharpshooters ·
Scongin's Georgia Battery*

Maney's Brigade Brig. Gen. George Maney
*1st-27th Tennessee · 6th-9th Tennessee · 24th Tennessee Battalion Sharpshooters ·
4th Tennessee (Provisional) · Smith's Mississippi Battery*

Wright's Brigade Brig. Gen. Marcus J. Wright
*8th Tennessee · 16th Tennessee · 28th Tennessee · 38th Tennessee · 51st-52nd Tennessee
Murray's Battalion Carnes' Tennessee Battery*

Strahl's Brigade Brig. Gen. Otho F. Strahl
4th-5th Tennessee · 19th Tennessee · 24th Tennessee · 31st Tennessee · 33rd Tennessee
Stanford's Mississippi Battery

Smith's Brigade Brig. Gen. Preston Smith, Col. Alfred J. Vaughn
11th Tennessee · 12th-47th Tennessee · 13th-154th Tennessee · 29th Tennessee
Dawson's Battalion Sharpshooters · Scott's Tennessee Battery

HINDMAN'S DIVISION Maj. Gen. Thomas C. Hindman, Brig. Gen. Patton Anderson
Anderson's Brigade Brig. Gen. Patton Anderson Col. J.H. Sharp
7th Mississippi · 9th Mississippi · 10th Mississippi · 41st Mississippi · 44th Mississippi
9th Mississippi · Battalion Sharpshooters · Garrity's Alabama Battery

Deas' Brigade Brig. Gen. Zachariah C. Deas
19th Alabama · 22nd Alabama · 25th Alabama · 39th Alabama · 50th Alabama
17th Alabama Sharpshooters · Dent's Alabama Battery

Manigault's Brigade Brig. Gen. Arthur Manigault
24th Alabama · 28th Alabama · 34th Alabama · 10th-19th South Carolina ·
Waters' Alabama Battery

HILL'S CORPS Lt. Gen. Daniel Harvey Hill
Escort *Raum's Company Georgia Cavalry*

BRECKINRIDGE'S DIVISION Maj. Gen. John C. Breckinridge
Adams' Brigade Brig. Gen. Daniel Adams
32nd Alabama · 13th-20th Louisiana · 16th-25th Louisiana · 19th Louisiana
Austin's Battalion Louisiana Sharpshooters · 5th Company Washington Artillery
Grave's Kentucky Battery

Helm's Brigade Brig. Gen. Benjamin Hardin Helm
41st Alabama · 2nd Kentucky · 4th Kentucky · 6th Kentucky · 9th Kentucky · Cobb's Kentucky Battery

Stovall's Brigade Brig. Gen, Marcellus Stovall
1st-3rd Florida · 4th Florida · 47th Georgia · 60th North Carolina · Mebane's Tennessee Battery

CLEBURNE'S DIVISION Maj. Gen. Patrick R. Cleburne
Polk's Brigade Brig. Gen. Lucius E. Polk
1st Arkansas · 3rd-5th Confederate · 2nd Tennessee · 35th Tennessee · 48th Tennessee
Helena (Ark) Light Artillery

Wood's Brigade Brig. Gen. Sterling Alexander Martin Wood
16th Alabama · 33rd Alabama · 45th Alabama · 18th Alabama Battalion
32nd-45th Mississippi · 15th Mississippi Sharpshooters · Semple's Alabama Battery

Deshler's Brigade Brig. Gen. James Deshler, Col. Roger Q. Mills
19th-24th Arkansas · 6th-10th-15th Texas · 17th-18th-24th-25th Texas Cavalry (Dismounted)
Dallas (TX) Light Artillery

WALKER'S RESERVE CORPS Maj. Gen. William Henry Talbot Walker
WALKER'S DIVISION Brig. Gen. States Rights Gist
Ector's Brigade Brig. Gen. Matthew D. Ector
29th North Carolina · 9th Texas · Pound's Mississippi Battalion · Stones' Alabama Battalion
10th Texas Cavalry (Dismounted) · 14th Texas Cavalry (Dismounted) · 32nd Texas Cavalry (Dismounted)

Wilson's Brigade Brig. Gen. Claudius Wilson
25th Georgia · 29th Georgia · 30th Georgia · 1st Georgia Sharpshooter Battalion
4th Louisiana Battalion · Howell's Georgia Battery

Gist's Brigade Col. Peyton Colquitt Liet. Col. Leroy Napier
46th Georgia · 8th Georgia Battalion · 24th South Carolina

LIDDELL'S DIVISION Brig. Gen. St. John Liddell
Liddell's Brigade Col. Daniel C. Govan
2nd-15th Arkansas · 6th-7th Arkansas · 5th-13th Arkansas · 8th Arkansas
1st Louisiana Regulars · Warren Light Artillery

Walthall's Brigade Brig. Gen. Edward Walthall
24th Mississippi · 27th Mississippi · 29th Mississippi · 30th Mississippi · 34th Mississippi
Fowler's Alabama Battery

BUCKNER'S CORPS Maj. Gen. Simon Bolivar Buckner
Escort *Clark's Company Tennessee Cavalry*

STEWART'S DIVISION Maj. Gen. Alexander P. Stewart
Clayton's Brigade Brig. Gen. Henry DeLamar Clayton
18th Alabama · 36th Alabama · 38th Alabama · 1st Arkansas Battery

Brown's Brigade Brig. Gen. John C. Brown
18th Tennessee · 26th Tennessee · 32nd Tennessee · 45th Tennessee
23rd Tennessee Battalion Sharpshooters · Dawson's Georgia Battery

Bate's Brigade Brig. Gen. William B. Bate
58th Alabama · 37th Georgia · 20th Tennessee · 15th-37th Tennessee
4th Georgia Battalion Sharpshooters · Eufaula Light Artillery

PRESTON'S DIVISION Brig. Gen. William Preston
Kelly's Brigade Brig. Gen. John Kelly
65th Georgia · 5th Kentucky · 58th North Carolina · 63rd Virginia

Trigg's Brigade Col. Robert C. Trigg
6th Florida · 7th Florida · 1st Florida Cavalry (Dismounted) · 54th Virginia

Gracie's Brigade Brig. Gen. Archibald Gracie Jr.
*1st Alabama Battalion · 2nd Alabama Battalion · 3rd Alabama Battalion ·
4th Alabama Heavy Artillery Battalion · 63rd Tennessee*

LONGSTREET'S FIRST CORPS
OF THE ARMY OF NORTHERN VIRGINIA Maj. Gen. John Bell Hood
JOHNSON'S PROVISIONAL DIVISION Brig. Gen. Bushrod R. Johnson
Johnson's Brigade Col. John S. Fulton
*17th Tennessee · 23rd Tennessee · 25th Tennessee · 44th Tennesee ·
9th Georgia Arillery, Company E*

Gregg's Brigade Brig. Gen. John Gregg Col. Cyrus A. Sugg
*3rd Tennessee · 10th Tennessee · 41st Tennessee · 50th Tennessee · 1st Tennessee Battalion
30th Tennessee · 7th Texas · Bledsoe's Missouri Battery*

McNair's Brigade Brig. Gen. Evander McNair Col. David Coleman
*1st Arkansas Mounted Rifles (Dismounted) · 2nd Arkansas Mounted Rifles (Dismounted)
25th Arkansas · 4th-31st-4th Battalion Arkansas · 39th North Carolina
Culpeper's South Carolina Battery*

HOOD'S DIVISION Brig. Gen. Evander M. Law
Robertson's Brigade Brig. Gen. Jerome Beverly Robertson Col. Van Manning
3rd Arkansas · 1st Texas · 4th Texas · 5th Texas

Benning's Brigade Brig. Gen. Henry L. Benning
2nd Georgia · 15th Georgia · 17th Georgia · 20th Georgia

Law's Brigade Col. James L. Sheffield
4th Alabama · 15th Alabama · 44th Alabama · 47th Alabama 48th Alabama

McLAW'S DIVISION Brig. Gen. Joseph B. Kershaw
Keshaw's Brigade Brig. Gen. Joseph B. Kershaw
*2nd South Carolina · 3rd South Carolina · 7th South Carolina · 8th South Carolina
15th South Carolina · 3rd South Carolina Battalion*

Humphrey's Brigade Brig. Gen. Benjamin G. Humphreys
13th Mississippi · 17th Mississippi · 18th Mississippi · 21st Mississippi

RESERVE ARTILLERY Major Felix Robertson
*Barret's Missouri Battery · Havis' Georgia Battery · Lumsden's Alabama Battery
Massenburg's Georgia Battery*

WHEELER'S CAVALRY CORPS Maj. Gen. Joseph Wheeler
WHARTON'S DIVISION Brig. Gen. John A. Wharton
Crew's Brigade Col. Constantine Crews
2nd Georgia · 3rd Georgia · 4th Georgia · Malone's Alabama Regiment

Harrison's Brigade Col. Thomas Harrison
*3rd Confederate · 3rd Kentucky · 4th Tennessee · 8th Texas (Terry's Texas Rangers) · 11th Texas
White's Tennessee Battery*

MARTIN'S DIVISION Brig. Gen. William T. Martin
Morgan's Brigade Col. John Tyler Morgan
1st Alabama · 3rd Alabama · 51st Alabama Partisan Rangers · 8th Confederate

Russell's Brigade Col. A.A. Russell
4th Alabama (Russell's) · 1st Confederate · Wiggin's Arkansas Battery

FORREST'S CAVALRY CORPS Brig. Gen. N. Bedford Forrest
ARMSTRONG'S DIVISION Brig. Gen. Frank Armstrong
Armstrong's Brigade Col. James T. Wheeler
3rd Arkansas · 2nd Kentucky · 6th Tennessee · 18th Tennessee Battalion

Dibrell's Brigade Col. George Dibrell
*4th Tennessee · 8th Tennessee · 9th Tennessee · 10th Tennessee · Huggins' Tennessee Battery
Morton's Tennessee Battery · Shaw's Tennessee Battalion*

PEGRAM'S DIVISION Brig. Gen. John Pegram
Davidson's Brigade Brig. Henry Davidson
*10th Confederate · 1st Georgia · 6th Georgia · 66th North Carolina · Rucker's Alabama Legion
Huwald's Battery*

Scott's Brigade Col. John S. Scott
*1st Louisiana · 2nd Tennessee · 5th Tennessee · Detachment of John Hunt Morgan's Command
Robinson's Louisiana Battery*

Suggested Reading

THE BATTLE OF CHICKAMAUGA

The Chickamauga Campaign (Glory or the Grave, A Mad Irregular Battle, and *Barren Victory)*
David A. Powell
Savas Beatie (2014)

A massive detailed study of the battle that will set the standard for Chickamauga studies. Powell adds even more to the understanding of the battle beyond what he has already contributed with his two previous works. Coming in three volumes, this will pretty much tell you everything you ever wanted to know about the battle.

Failure in the Saddle: Nathan Bedford Forrest, Joseph Wheeler, and the Confederate Cavalry in the Chickamauga Campaign
David A. Powell
Savas Beatie (2010)
ISBN 978-1-932714-87-6

A detailed study of the role of the Confederate Cavalry in the Chickamauga campaign and how, despite the legends, it failed repeatedly in its mission to be the eyes and ears of the army. Powell challenges many myths relating to the mounted arm in this campaign.

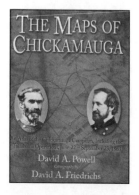

The Maps of Chickamauga: An Atlas of the Chickamauga Campaign, Including the Tullahoma Operations, June 22 - September 23, 1863
David A. Powell
Savas Beatie (2009)
ISBN 978-1932714-72-2

A detailed study of all the moves of the campaign and battle of Chickamauga. For a battle that was confusing on many levels, this book details the fine points and helps even the expert learn something new.

Chickamauga and Chattanooga
Theodore Savas, editor
Civil War Regiments book issue, Vol. 7, No. 1
Regimental Studies, Inc. (paperback, 2000)

A wonderful collection of original essays on a variety of
subjects related to both the battles of Chickamauga and
Chattanooga. Topics include the battle of Missionary
Ridge, the United States Regular Brigade, Patrick
Cleburne's defense of Tunnel Hill, the 2nd Georgia
Battalion Sharpshooters, and Camp Thomas during the
Spanish American War.

The Chickamauga Campaign
Steven E. Woodworth, editor
Southern Illinois University Press (2010)
ISBN 978-0-8093-2980-9

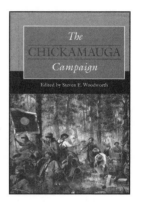

Woodworth collects a number of essays from an
impressive array of authors, dealing with a wide
variety of different topics. For those who know the
story of the battle, this delivers details that are new
and add different perspectives: Thomas Crittenden
and Alexander McCook, the Confederate leadership
at McClemore's Cove, D. H. Hill, A. P. Stewart's
breakthrough, Cleburne's night attack, Longstreet's
role on September 20, Negley on Snodgrass Hill, and
the establishment of Chickamauga as the first National
Military Park.

Six Armies in Tennessee
Steven E. Woodworth
University of Nebraska Press (1999)
ISBN 978-0803298-13-2

Woodworth presents a highly readable study of the
Tullahoma, Chickamauga, Chattanooga, and Knoxville
Campaigns that also does an excellent job of placing
them in the bigger picture of the Civil War. An
excellent account of the struggle for East Tennessee in
1863.

About the Author

William Lee White is a park ranger at the Chickamauga and Chattanooga National Military Park, where he gives tours and other programs at the Chickamauga and Lookout Mountain battlefields. He is the author of several articles and essays on topics related to the Western Theater and the editor of *Great Things Are Expected of Us: The Letters of Colonel C. Irvine Walker, 10th South Carolina Infantry CSA*. Over the years, he has spoken to many roundtables, historical societies, and other history-minded groups.

EMERGING CIVIL WAR SERIES